"From Living to Legacy"
Beyond the Barriers of Mediocrity
by
Donelle Cole

From Living to Legacy
Donelle Cole
Copyright © 2019 by Donelle Cole

ISBN 978-1-7341077-0-8

Edited by The Haven Publishing, Minneapolis, MN

THE Haven PUBLISHING

Praise for *From Living to Legacy*

"Energy! That is what you will walk away with every time you read this book. Donelle is inspiring people from all walks of life with some of the most relevant ideas for living wisely! Every page has something you haven't heard quite the way you're reading it now. Few publications have the fresh ingredients this manual for success has. It truly is the perfect balance of information and revelation!"

-Dr. Charles Martin

"As an author and writing coach I am elated to present this body of work. This book is a timeless piece that will live on for generations. In this riveting and transparent body of work, Donelle calls people to their highest and greatest selves. Leaders, professionals, laymen and women, and individuals are made aware of their frailties as he emboldens and empowers them. Donelle guides readers with examples from his own journey. He presents his own past despair, childhood, and traumatic experiences for readers to master their lives with purpose! From Living to Legacy is an eloquent resource that speaks directly to the heart while creating transformation in the mind. Sit back, relax and be prepared to be challenged to build the life you've always hoped and dreamed for!"

-Anesha A. Sharp, Author and Book Coach

Acknowledgements

First and foremost, I give honor to God for the many blessings that have been cultivated in my life. Thank you to the many individuals that made this project possible: my book coach Anesha Alexandria, editor De'Vonna Pittman, graphic designer Nanjar Tri Mukti, photographer Eric Hardaway, mentor Keith Boutwell, Cody Madison, Radhika Cruz for insight, and Jenni Reavis for sending me research information while hosting lectures overseas. Lord knows I can't put a price on the sacrifice you all made.

I'm super grateful for my wife Elizabeth Cole, for allowing me to "pick her brain". I want to give a special salute to my four daughters, Destynee who advised me to write a book, Keayanna, Daejah, and Heaven. I would like to extend a special thanks to my mother Karen for her relentless love and compassion. Without you all, there would be no me. I'm forever indebted to every mentor that poured countless energy into my future, and spent many years investing in me. Thank you for every prayer, word of encouragement, and every comedic gesture. I'm grateful that you taught me to appreciate my flaws and to embrace a life I never imagined I could have for myself and my family.

Table of contents

Chapter One-The Barriers of a Broken Identity 6

Chapter Two: The Barriers of a Broken Vision 65

Chapter Three–The Barriers of a Broken Mindset 91

Chapter Four-The Barriers of Broken Emotions 117

Chapter Five: Principle of Intentionality 147

Chapter Six-The Power of Newness 155

Chapter Seven: Living the Legacy 171

Notes and appendix 181

Foot notes   188

About the Author 190

Preface

Thank you for your support in the purchasing on my first book, "From Living to Legacy." If you are looking for a body of work that will challenge every paradigm that limits your potential, you have come to the right place. Let me be the first to thank you for taking control of your destiny. Many are called, but few are chosen. I am honored to have the privilege of pouring into your greatness.

This book, "From Living to Legacy" came about as I was forced to face many of the flawed beliefs that restricted my own state of evolution. Just like you I have lived a long life aspired by those who grew beyond the norms to create extraordinary lives. Unfortunately this reality isn't the story or narrative that we all get to experience. I am a product of the inner city. I have a brother that died at the age of seventeen to gun violence. I have another brother serving forty years in prison. I have lost three friends to drug overdoses in the past five years. Truthfully, I am a man that had to fall in love with the ideal of being uncomfortable, to surpass the common mishaps that was embedded in the foundation of my life.

With that stated, we are going to go on a journey that will navigate us from simply living and merely existing to leaving a legacy and of course, living with intention and purpose. In the pages to follow, we will examine two life principles, adapting to mediocrity or adopting to mindfulness. Hang on to your future, let go of your past. Your life will never be the same after reading this.

Your path to greatness begins now — the only thing you need to bring is your determination for a divine destination. I will pack (or unpack) the rest. Prepare to change your trajectory from simply living, to leaving a legacy.

Why are we changing?
Do you think we settle for far less than we are capable of achieving? Of course! Even in the land of abundance more people today are disengaged than ever before in history. Every one of us was created with the ability to achieve far more than we could ever imagine, yet a majority of us die before ever scratching the surface of our dreams. In many cases our potential is robbed by fear and limiting self-beliefs we decide to feed into. My goal is to help you clearly define the states of mediocrity that is challenging your evolution and to help you overcome these barriers.

How will we get there?

I will introduce bullet proof strategies that I have acquired from some of the brightest, toughest, and most effective leaders. All of these things have contributed to my growth. I will also include footnotes along with supporting material for those of you who desire to dive deeper into advanced exploration. There is also a workbook for those who like to go above and beyond. The summary and breakdown of material is as followed:

Section One: From Living - Bound by Barriers: Four Barriers to Mediocrity

Chapter One: The Barrier of identity. Get clear on who you are called to become. Acquire clarity on authenticity.

This will occur in five pillars:

Define: How do you define yourself?
Discover: Where are you gifted and what is your element?
Dysfunction: What identity thefts are robbing you of your defined excellence?

Dissect: Distinguish which behaviors align with who you want to become versus what you need to leave behind.
Design: Align who you are with the divine origin of who God says you are.

Chapter Two: The Barrier of Vision. This will involve defining what scope of vision draws upon your greatest aspirations. What type of visions are limiting your progression? We will also dive into some strategies that were used by creators and we will discuss how they leveraged their own imagination to move from mediocrity. When we come from a broken image, we have a broken vision for our lives. We will reshape your perspective for success. As you change your image, your vision must change also. Next, we'll discuss mindsets.

Chapter Three: The Barriers of a Broken Mindset. In the journey through mindset, we will evaluate and take inventory of our belief systems. We will compare mindsets, mentalities, and limiting beliefs. We will analyze what type of factors are embedded in the conscious mind and why is it difficult to move forward. This will require us to become vulnerable about misconceptions that keep us stagnant in life.

Chapter Four: The Barriers of Emotional Turmoil: We will explore the emotional disruption of challenging beliefs within our mindsets. Emotions tend to rule who we are so in order to achieve more, we must have a consciousness of how emotions contribute or deter us from our best efforts.

Intersession: By aligning your identity, vision, thoughts, and emotions with the ideal direction that you desire for your life to reflect, you will achieve optimal results.

Within these chapters you will become enlightened and equipped. Chapter five through seven are about becoming intentional while living your legacy.

Section Two: To Legacy - Found by faithfulness: delivered by empowerment.

Chapter Five: Principle of Intentionality: We will now explore the power of being intentional. This involves accountability and stewardship of our identities, vision, mindsets, and emotions. As we channel these four paradigms towards a vision we explore the power of newness. This also require eliminating everything that is counterintuitive or not in alignment with your higher self. We will take a look at being focused, specific, and grounded on a foundation of excellence. Remember if you're called for more, "Don't decorate your cubicle."

Chapter Six: The power of Newness: The power of newness is walking in your defined destination. This section requires creating a paradigm through new rituals. As we complete resetting new conditioned beliefs, we head into our final chapter, "Living the legacy."

Chapter Seven: Living the Legacy: This is where expectation meets reality. We will take a hard look at what we want to become, and what God desires for our lives. This is where we eliminate the factors that come between these associations. As we conclude the journey you will become enlightened, empowered, and equipped to live out your greatest authenticity or shall I say, our authentic self. The reason why most people are unfulfilled is because they have found comfort pursuing everything except the reason they were called here on Earth.

Introduction

All of the things I've been through brings back memories, memories that arise in the forefront of my brain constantly. One conversation went something like this…

"Hey what's up fam, my name is Donelle!"
"I know your name, I'm your uncle Charles," he said, extending his hand out to give me dap. It was an awkward introduction.
"I live in Texas now, but I met you when you were about five years old you've grown up a lot,"
"Oh okay cool, Yeah I'm fourteen now," thinking this dude must be a blood (gang member). I winked to my mom, but she looked back at me foolishly with that "telekinetic black mama" shut yo' mouth look.

Picture this. He was wearing a super long 3X bright red Dickies t-shirt, red Dickie pants, and with red Chuck Taylor shoes along with the real obvious giveaway.... red shoes laces! He was about six feet tall, light complexion, well defined cheek bones, with a slight gash on his cheek. The tattoos that read "Blood gang" were deeply engraved into his skin. I mean, who wears all that red on the east side of Oklahoma. No one went out of their way to dress like that without intentions of proving a point. I could tell my mother was excited to see him, so I just acted naive to keep from getting in trouble.

"We headed to the store to get y'all some candy, yelled my mom, watch your cousin while we are gone and we'll bring y'all back some candy." "Yes mam," my brothers and I responded. Let's get some swishes too she said to my uncle in a whisper as the door closed.

My uncle Charles had left his son with us. I was the oldest sibling of two brothers which automatically promoted me to the "Man of the house". This is what happens when you're raised by a single mother in the hood on welfare. We were accustomed to poverty. Eviction notices, domestic violence, substance abuse, you name it, we have been there and seen it. Even teen pregnancy. My mother, a high school star athlete dropped out of the tenth grade after getting pregnant with me at age 14. My father was as vacant as the void in my heart, but that's another story.

For some reason I loved the drama. I had a deep attraction to dysfunction. It was like I signed up for the "BS" if you know what I mean. I got into so much trouble in Tulsa that we had to move over a hundred miles away to Oklahoma City to my grandma's house. It was six of us in a two-bedroom house. I looked over at newly acquainted cousin from Texas, he was about ten yrs. old.

I said" Hey what's up fam, ya dad a blood huh?"
"What you mean by that bro?" he responded
"I'm saying he *flamed up*" you see all that red he is wearing?" I said.
"Nah, he just like red, that's all."

I could tell from my cousin's body language something was off. You know that awkward silence. It's a dead giveaway when someone is trying to cover up something. Yeah it felt like that. Then all of a sudden, a loud bang emerged from the front-room. I overhead my mother screaming, "Mama come here now! Hurry please! Get in the car! Please hurry!" I rushed to see what happened and they pushed me back, ran out the door and slammed the door behind them.

Fifteen to twenty minutes later they came back in the front door startled. We were still in the back room. I opened the door to see what happened. They were covered in blood. Blood was all over my mom, her shoes, shirts, pants and on her face and hands. My grandma was covered as well. "Close the door and stay in the room Donelle!" my mother yelled frantically. I opened the door anyway. Shrewd terror covered her face as she stood there motionless. She was petrified. I had never seen her this alarmed before. She pulled my cousin out and closed the door behind him trying to keep everyone else from noticing.

"What happened?" my brothers asked me. "Real talk bro, I don't know, but there was blood everywhere. I'm not staying in here." I ran out to see my grandma and my mother. Tears fell, they were crying profusely. We later found out that the uncle we had just seen had been shot dead. We had so much excitement and were just waiting for candy and to catch up on old memories, and now…he was dead. He had been killed because of the color of his clothing. As he was walking out of the store a teenage Crip pulled out a gun and shot him in the neck and chest. My mother ran to pick my uncle up from the ground but couldn't stop the bleeding. The gash in his neck was too deep. She ran to get my grandmother, we only lived about two hundred feet from the store. By the time my grandmother made it back to the store he was dead. My grandmother sat there staring at his body in disbelief, she could not believe what had just happened.

They had nightmares for months. "You'll either end up dead or in jail," is what they told me. You see, as much as tried to deny it, I knew what my uncle was about, because I followed in his footsteps. We were taught penitentiary chances were better than living in poverty. We were encouraged to resent the fathers that abandoned us. Somehow, we were even taught to settle for far beneath our greatest aspirations. We were taught to suppress pain. Where I come from dreams are a myth so we settle for mediocrity. And that results in a myriad of other things.

I was a stubborn juvenile on the detention show "Scared Straight." My brother died to gun violence at the age of eighteen, and my other brother is serving forty years in prison. But, for me… somehow God showed up with phenomenal grace. A grace that shifted my journey from selling dope in the streets to living a life far beyond what I could imagine for myself. I am now married to an incredible woman, I have multiple businesses, and I am making an impact in my community.

I have learned that there are some people in the world who are merely living to get by, and there are others who are building legacies. Each of us have our own set of challenges, but the level at which you overcome, is what you will be defined by. My goal is to show you how to overcome mediocrity. Let me take you on a journey to tell you what I didn't know.

Identity poem

If only I were raised by Andrew Carnegie, my wealth of knowledge would surely soar
Napoleon Hill would be my counselor to teach me purpose, a focal point
To mold my greatness by Oprah Winfrey
Maya Angelou would open all the doors to
Mighty precepts within my conscious changed my life forever more
The streets taught me that life is tough, Les Brown said there's more in store
John C Maxwell showed me God, like Dr. Myles… the great Monroe
If Coretta Scott were my mother, I would have learned to be a King
Warren Buffet would teach me stock to leverage wealth for greater things
If John F Kennedy was my father, in leadership I would excel
I'd fight for freedom like Mandela who taught me we can change the world
If Steve Biko was my mentor I would have learned to love my skin
He said black is beautiful, and let the light lead within
If Dr. Wayne molded me I would have been forever young
He taught me life is but a vapor and to seek the things that bring you joy
Grant Cardone would teach me business and to build tenacity when I needed strength
Joel Osteen would give perspective, to fight like King David did
Jim Rohn taught the art of wealth, and how to break the mold of scarcity
I was raised with lack of faith and the mental state of poverty
Everywhere I searched for you, it's true I did, but you could not find me
After finding everyone else… still I lacked identity

Chapter One-The Barriers of a Broken Identity

First Barrier to Mediocrity: Lack of Identity

We were born to a system that designed us to fail but born with an identity that designed us to conquer.

During my enlistment in the United States Navy, whenever I came home, my family and friends marveled over the gifts I brought back. Whether my travels were to Australia, Singapore, Guam, or Japan, one thing was for sure, I always brought home something people in Oklahoma had never seen before. Considering we didn't travel much growing up, we were accustomed to having a similar sense of fashion. Everyone dressed the same.

When I made it home, my little brothers were the first to invade my stash and go through all of my gear. There were these very *special* limited-edition Nike shoes that I loved. The first time I saw them, I had to get them. Maybe, it was the fact that I grew up broke that fueled my enthusiasm. Either way, I just had to have them.

Every time I wore those shoes, the reaction was almost immediate from people that checked them out. People questioned where I bought them, and how they could get some for themselves. Of course, I would tell them they were custom made, and that they wouldn't be able to find another pair like them. What was so astonishing about those shoes? Well, they were extremely rare and most importantly they were authentic. They were original. No one else on the planet had these exact same shoes.

Just like the shoes in this example, each of us are custom made. Each of us are distinctly created and distinguished by design according to a mighty purpose. When you were created there was a need for you on the earth. There was a void. This void was so vast that God could only create you *in His image* to fill it. Mediocrity was never in His plan, even though many of us have subjected ourselves to just that. My goal is to encourage you to find out what the world's void is without you. Why were you needed on earth?

If you are a sneaker-head you are aware of the price people will pay for rare shoes. It's like any other rare commodity, it holds the most value. Oil, gold, water, gas and land are very rare because they can't be remanufactured, and you know what…God only created one you. Somehow and somewhere this concept of mediocrity influenced us to believe otherwise.

In life, we all experience extreme highs and lows, so you and I are no strangers to the burdens of life. For the masses, these burdens have stopped many from pursuing all they are called to achieve in which I call the "barriers to mediocrity." This perception of reality influences us to have dreams that are untouched or unexplored. It causes us to have a flawed and very limited scope of one's self compared to the aspirations God shaped us for. I will provide a different perspective and a meaning for why you were created.

Everyday many of us are represented by different versions of ourselves, personas. We must present those personas to the world every single day in one form or another. Many of us have a persona that is *lazy*. This version has no desire to put effort into anything. Then, there's the part of us that is fearful and abandons any form of growth. This side of us will do anything to keep from standing out in a world that thrives on conformity. Then there is the insecure side of us that feels unworthy of success.

Although all of these perceptions exist, there is a side that longs to see dreams fulfilled. Within the context of all of these versions, nothing overpowers the fact that God designed you to be phenomenal. Everyone is born with the potential to be great, to be valued and to play a significant role in the world, however many of us (yes, this too includes me) have been conditioned to have mediocre relationships, jobs, and standards of living. This is where the problems arise. This sort of conditioning has trickled down for many generations. Regardless of the lack of cultural heritage, cultural bias, social norms, behavioral patterns, or stereotypical stigmas, nothing should be able to limit our capacity to thrive. When it does, we are living in a state of mediocrity.

In my lifetime I have seen some of the most capable individuals robbed of the ideal life, one that God intended for them to experience. I too, was among those individuals. My state of conditioning was a result of a deprived mindset adopted while in my youth. *When mediocrity or the state of being mediocre becomes the standard in life, someone or something has convinced us to leave the better version of ourselves on the backburner*. Settling for mediocrity is like relinquishing authority you never knew you had.

What does identity mean to you?

---

*The process of becoming
mediocre begins when a
person lacks identity*

From the day we are born, there are many factors
that are fighting to shape and define just who we are.
From the color of our skin, the amount of income we
make, the opinions and beliefs we agree or disagree
upon, to the environments we live in, there is a
preconceived idea that fights to conceptualize who or
what we are. One thought I want to challenge you with
in this chapter is, who defined you and what you are
capable of achieving for your life.

The process of becoming mediocre begins when a
person lacks identity. Where there's no identity, there's
no purpose. Where there is no purpose, there is no
meaning. If there is no meaning, then why does one
even exist? Identity is defined as the condition or
character, who a person or thing is, their qualities,
beliefs, etc., that distinguishes them from another person
or thing. The foundation for overcoming mediocrity
starts with recognizing your own uniqueness. Your
uniqueness is dependent upon your identity. The cliché,
"you can be whatever you want to be" comes down to
this vital point, your life is a reflection of who you are
and the choices you have made. Who we feel we are
dictates the actions we take in life. This is a universal
principle that applies to all areas of life: business,

personal, relational, and spiritual. This is also the same in regards to a position or title an individual occupies. You can be an entrepreneur, CEO of a major company, a college student, doctor, lawyer, or pastor of a church. You can be a mother, father or a child, what I said, still holds true. The beliefs you have about your identity will dictate the outcome your life.

Who defined your sense of identity? As a young naive enthusiast raised around individuals who were not educated, yet had the highest incarceration rate, I began to question which factors contributed to these *common* realities. Rather through tradition or cultural traits we tend to adopt certain patterns that contribute to the molding or shaping of who we will become. I have been considered inferior, lazy, "at-risk," and a thug. All of these factors equate to a destiny that is far beneath my greatest aspirations. Research shows just how impressionable and susceptible the mind is. We know its power to influence so many of us who were bound to mediocrity far before we ever realized it. These conditions promote the mental deficiencies that limit the likelihood of us thriving or succeeding.

If there was a lesson that I wish I understood early on in life it would be the significance of identity, and that if cultivated it would produce exuberant results. ***By choosing the best version of yourself you are allowed to dictate the narrative of your life.*** I want you to understand your uniqueness is necessary to anyone you come in contact with. Since a void in the Earth led to the creation of your existence, it's your divine duty to find out what that void is.

The universe caters to us based on our state of consciousness and the identity we choose. There are many adversities that each of us will face. We often fail to overcome or confront our "inner critic." That inner critic is fueled by mediocrity.

Mediocrity in itself is a form of oppression. It suppresses the desire to explore greater potential. Greater potential is a higher sense of your identity. If you don't define your purpose for being on the earth, you will be like a plane that never leaves the flight deck. What good is a plane that never leaves the flight deck? It looks good on the outside, but the reality is, you will never know the potential because it isn't performing, nor doing what it was created to do. You have the potential to fly, but if you continue to live a life of mediocrity, you won't ever take-off.

Pillar One: Define-who you are called to become

Without self-actualization (knowledge of self) you can't reach your full potential nor lead others to theirs. This is why people continue to live beneath their true potential. What are your values and principles? What foundation are you built on? By definition of identity--- our greatest aspirations are found when we finally realize who we are created to be, and fight to become it. Without a doubt God created you to be dope.

There are many factors that define us as individuals. Some people are defined by religion, their hopes and aspirations are guided by principles of godliness. Some people are defined by material things, their whole façade is based on the accumulation of wealth and fame. Some people are defined by their careers. They deeply immerse themselves in their life's obsessions. Others have ways in which they define themselves as well rather political affiliations, family, etc. With respect to all of these examples, one thing rings true, we subconsciously define ourselves by what we value most. What you value most is exemplified through the actions of your heart.

So, how do you define yourself? Some people define themselves by the characteristics of the environments they were raised in. But, there are those who design the ideal perception of who they want to become, and they become just that. My goal is to challenge you with the same approach.

Every day we are faced with an internal conflictions of multiple states of consciousness. Sometimes the battle is won by the best versions of ourselves. Our days are ruled by a fierce sense of clarity, victory, and hope to achieve greater things. Other times we lose the battle to lower states of consciousness. In these lower states we become diluted by our own oblivion, and we are blinded by our lack of mindfulness. We end up sacrificing our destinies and succumbing to fear, insecurities, self-doubt, lack of growth and other variables that suppress greatness. Each of those factors produces a desired outcome that is governed by our belief system. Rather you believe you were created for purpose or lack you must confront the basis of what governs your identity. Each one of us is a mirror-reflection of the programming that conditions us. This programming defines our standards.

As an adolescent, we have limited control on the decisions that form our lives. Most things are simply not within our control. We don't get to choose what race, education, economic stance, or our parents when we are born. We hopelessly and sometimes dreadfully accept any and every state of influence fed to us by culture and society. The outcome in our lives are a direct result of situations we've been born in to. Just as seeds bear the same fruit it comes from, we too flourish based on what is beneath our own surface.

In most cases, it isn't the lack of opportunities that lead us toward a life of mediocrity. The culprit is a lack of belief in who we are called to become, that prevents us from pursuing our greatest call. Therefore, the first step to overcoming mediocrity is awareness.

Who are some of your heroes?

In life, we all have idols and heroes that we naturally gravitate towards. There's something about their beliefs we find appealing. Their courage to be influential, bold, persistent, or their tenacity to overcome despite adversity, are reasons we admire them. The philosophies we adopt mentally govern what we value and how we think. We are entirely made up of the things we believe in.

Sometimes we subconsciously acquire a sense of who we are from modeled beliefs. Modeled examples can lead you down the wrong path to brokenness. It can also lead you to cultivate dormant aspirations you may have never knew existed. The story of Bantu is a prime example.

Stephen Bantu Biko[1], a revolutionary activist in South Africa, was recognized for saying "poverty is a mindset." He also coined the term "Black Consciousness," a philosophy that inspired minorities to no longer perceive themselves as inferior to other cultures. He believed each of us has a personal accountability to rightfully live out our legitimate position in the world. But there was a problem, his philosophies didn't align with the beliefs people had about themselves. Oppression was so deeply ingrained in the citizens that they perceived themselves as inadequate.

For this reason, they governed themselves by lower states of consciousness. Murder plagued the streets, people killed themselves and others. Parties and drunkenness were as common as festivals in the summer time. No one had a desire for economic growth or prosperity, and education was flawed. Even worse, self-hatred was a basis of their foundation.

How many of us can relate to this state of conditioning right now? Though many enslaved people had

---

[1] Steve Biko – Biography https://www.biography.com/people/steve-biko-38884 I placed this in order to show how beliefs shape identity and how modeled examples shift behavior, action, and attitudes.

become free physically, mentally they had no will power, knowledge, or intellect on how to overcome these stigmas.

Biko and his team of leaders sparked a revolution, they created change by targeting the belief system of each individual. Negative connotations were associated with anything black or anyone black. Since people were conditioned that way, Biko began associating the term "black" with things of beauty, power, love, intelligence and resilience. By taking this stance it allowed citizens to evaluate the perception of how they viewed themselves in regards to culture.

"Black Consciousness" was a philosophy that challenged "self-awareness." Meaning this challenged the way each individual "defined" themselves. Not only did Biko's vision challenge the way they thought, but it challenged the way they lived. He taught a generation of people how to abolish a poor and oppressive perception of themselves.

During this period when the colored South Africans were deeply oppressed by colonizers, he looked at the citizens and recognized a need. There was a void. The education system instituted beliefs that encouraged them to remain victims. South Africans weren't taught how to become self-sufficient, they didn't know how or where to attain food. Biko realized relying on the government was man's biggest weakness, and as the people began to build, their society began to thrive.

When the Black South Africans couldn't find jobs, Biko *empowered them to create.* He taught the people how to build hospitals, so they would have healthcare. He taught them how to build schools to educate themselves. He reformed education while introducing leaders that looked like them. By taking this approach they were able to *emulate leaders of a higher consciousness,* and they were able to *evolve from their belief systems.* They were able to envision their capability to be so much *more*...doctors, lawyers, and teachers. By radically disengaging traditional methodologies, and letting go of old beliefs they were able to adopt new mental programming. Bikos' job was far from complete, he taught his people the process of vegetation including how to grow crops and feed themselves. When oppressors grew violent he channeled his energy towards building progress through self-discipline and character. He incorporated the art of compassion and self-love to stop people from killing each other, and to create healthy environments that promoted love and prosperity.

As the transition occurred, each man and woman gravitated towards a higher version of themselves. This allowed them to go from merely living, to building a legacy. None of that was possible until they confronted the ugly truth about what had been ingrained in their belief system and ultimately shifted their identity.

Rites of passage

Rites of passage[2] played a key role in our primal instinctual make up. And though each stage of life presents distinct challenges, we were birthed with the innate ability to overcome any challenge. In early society, as hunters and gatherers our survival was dependent upon our ability to have security, protection, and food. The animalistic behaviors of human nature prevailed as our genetic uniqueness made us a dominant species.

Rites of passage fulfilled an important premise of our biology. Though we are wired to seek comfort, our primal instinct and biology is wired for the pursuit of achievement.

Transitioning from survivor to being *comfortable* has become the social norm. We have all but abandoned a key factor that shaped our evolution. Rites of passage wasn't just a "pat-on-the-back, rah-rah good game sport to

---

[2] Rites of passage acknowledges how transitional periods contribute to states of identity. Joining certain societal expectations has even be known to contribute to cognitive dissonance. See reference for more information.

congratulate the efforts of success, it was a monument to celebrate the molding of identity. Identity drives the narrative of our conditioned progress or lack thereof.

As noted in the story about Biko, our sense of identity is cultivated by what has our attention. Biko introduced a *disruption* that challenged the roots and depth of who they believed they were. Each stage of evolution is a rite of passage. May this material be a disruption that challenges the mediocre traits fighting to hold you captive.

Four important traits found in the rite of passage:

1. Building a foundation
2. Understanding roles in relationships
3. Preserving traditional values that were handed down
4. Strengthening beliefs or reframing beliefs through *upgraded* programming
5. Helping others to understand their purpose.

What narrative is contributing to your identity? Each one of these factors play a critical role in the shaping of our identities. From the foundation, to social intelligence and our role in relationships, value and character, and also your purpose and meaning for living. As we continue to explore, my focus is to both help you build self-awareness and to guide you. I want to ensure that you are clearly defining how these four factors will help you grow.

Action Plan

1. Define your foundation. What type of individual do you want to become? If you committed to the best version of yourself, what type of life would you have?

2. How do you view yourself in regards to relationships? Do you have an inferiority complex like the illustration

and story of Bantu? What are some factors limiting your evolution?

3. What type of values do you have that are limiting your growth?

4. What is your purpose in life (what gives you a sense of value and fulfillment)?

Pillar Two: Discovery your own uniqueness.
Where is your gifts? What is your element?

I am a brother of three that comes from a family of trash talk. My brothers and I were commonly known for our notorious clown sessions. We spent hours clowning each other with the most degrading insults we could think of. Sometimes the insults were funny, but other times we went overboard. The goal with going overboard meant touching the most sensitive areas that caused the most emotional pain. Whoever could do that, had successfully won.

It's one thing to clown about wearing raggedy shoes, but it is another thing to clown about the loss of a loved one, the pain of facing abuse or rejection from an absent parent. We had so many incredible gifts and aspirations, however, we excelled at the *inner critic.* We spent a lot of time trying to make each other feel bad, because we all felt bad about our own selves. That is what the common rag sessions were about, no matter how well we did in life, there would always be something we could find wrong in ourselves and others.

I remember going on a Key Club retreat in the fourth grade in school. I had on a pair of wrangler jeans and a sweat shirt that was two sizes too big. My mother always bought our clothes extra-large so it took a little time to outgrow them. I felt so embarrassed that I decided to clown myself as a means of laughing to connect with others. The truth is, I was insecure and didn't feel I fit in.

At the event we had a contest, and I was extremely excited and nervous at the same time. We had to write a speech about our teams. Whoever wrote the best speech won the contest. This came as an easy "A" for me because I was accustomed to noticing things about others. Out of all the members that wrote speeches, I was selected to present.

When I stepped on stage to give my speech I was nervous, "What if they laugh at me or what if I get booed off stage? What if I perspire and people point at my arm pit stains? What if?" Now, I think how come we don't use "what ifs" as a positive? Like, what if I killed this speech and someone creates a statue about how moving it was? That would be incredible right?

As I approached the podium my knees began to shake like an earthquake in a valley. Apparently, I was crazy nervous, but I continued to the microphone as my team applauded. The conductor handed me the mic. I looked out at the crowed, and everyone got quiet. After stumbling over the first few words I mentioned each member on my team by their distinguishing traits that made them unique. Afterwards, I delivered a heartfelt message about how important each member was to our team. Instead of using insults I defined them by their potential. They were all gifted. God created each of us with some incredible abilities. This only becomes clear through self-discovery.

Many of us possess phenomenal qualities that were given to us at birth. Some gifts take time to develop while others occur naturally. You may be gifted in art, communication, organization, leadership, athletics, music, etc. Each gift that God gives you is an extension of your identity. God designed each of us with something that should makes us feel alive. I like to refer to it as your "lane or element." It's crazy just how much time people spend investing in everything that drains their enthusiasm for life.

Think about it, most of us work at jobs we dread. Some of us are in relationships that are dead. Some of us have finances that don't have two legs to stand on, and a majority of us have dreams that don't get of bed. That means the only time we see our dreams are when we are asleep. There has to be more to life than this.

"Most of us work jobs we dread. Some are in relationships that are dead. Some of us have finances that don't have two legs.........to stand on. And a majority of us have dreams that won't get out of bed. That means the only time we see our dreams are when we are sleep. There has to be more to life than this."

I want you to be inspired to evaluate the uniqueness in how you are wired. By understanding how you are wired you can maneuver self-limiting beliefs that are standing between you and your evolution. Your uniqueness is your superpower to the world. Often times, social conformity suppresses who we are, but when we indulge in self-discovery we find our uniqueness. Just like Gillian Lynne[3] did. As a young child she had many struggles, and found it hard to focus her attention unlike other students in the class. Some called it hyperactivity or ADHD. The condition became so overwhelming that the students and teachers began scrutinizing the young talent.

Her mother couldn't explain why her daughter was so disruptive during class. The high energy, passionate, and overzealous behavior illustrated from the young child was viewed as unacceptable. The teachers found the annoyance unbearable, and she was reprimanded and sent to a psychiatrist.
"She is very disruptive and needs to be placed on meds," the teachers said. Following the advice given by the teachers, the mother quickly disclosed the symptoms to the psychiatrist. "She doesn't sit still in class. Her behavior is erratic. She has become a disturbance that the teachers can no longer deal with."
After careful evaluation the doctor asked if the mother could leave the room momentarily so he could find out how to help her.

As the music played in the background the doctor noticed Gillian's attention shift dramatically. The twitching in her fingers grew erratic. The more she attempted to restrain herself to the seat, the more anxious she became.

---

[3] Gillian Lynne struggle to focus was believed to have been a mental issue. The doctor revealed that she was able to think better by moving. Her identity could have been severely suppressed based on the doctor diagnosis.

The doctor began to recognize how enthusiastic she moved to the music being played in the background. After careful consideration he adjusted the volume louder. Next, he paid close attention to her body language. Finally, he asked Gillian if she could get out of the seat and dance. The young talent moved with elegance, as if she was created for music, and music alone. It was as if she had felt love for the first time. The vibrations of harmony were soothing to her soul. It was at this moment the doctor noticed the erratic behavior being displayed was due to her passion and joy for music.

The child didn't have any mental issues at all, what she had was a natural gift that had been misunderstood by those around her. The psychiatrist recommended Gillian's mother place her in dancing classes, and she did just that. As she joined the dancing classes she advanced quickly. The teachers and other students took note of how natural the composition of music was to her. They were all impressed by the natural aptitude to grasp the concepts so quickly. At her previous school Gillian didn't fit in, but dance school sparked her enthusiasm. Most importantly, she was in her element.

The young girl that had been ridiculed by teachers had become one of the most influential names in the music. This journey led to her founding one of the most prominent dance studios in the world, the Gillian Art School of Opera. This story expresses just how deep our gifts can be tied to who we are called to become. Gillian's legacy and contribution was deeply tied to the gifts within her. This is the power of identity.

There is a free personality assessment at the end of the book in Appendix A. Take the assessments and compare them to where you are in your life cycle. Are you currently in your element of passion or are you living in a life that is draining your enthusiasm?

Know Thyself: Invest in Self-Discovery

The most empowering state that we can take advantage of in life occurs by identifying who we are. Oprah found her niche in communication, Martin Luther King Jr. found his in influence, John C. Maxwell realized he was an expert in leadership, Nikola Tesla knew he would thrive in creating inventions. We all have particular abilities that we advance at fairly well. We are usually influenced in society to find identity through labels. Taking time to evaluate how you can complement culture invites the world into your own distinct uniqueness.

Do you remember the cliques in school? They included, the popular in-crowd, hipsters, athletes, geeks and nerds who flexed their sense of purpose based on intellect or of course, gangsters or religious folks. If you couldn't blend in with any of these social groups you probably had a difficult time with a sense of identity. Then as we mature, our identity can take many forms. Sometimes we become who our parents want us to become as a means of acquiring acceptance. We decide on the career or job that best suits their interest. We follow and attain education based on what is taught in school. We follow the advice of friends and family, etc. or of course, television, social media, magazines, etc.

If we didn't find the type of healthy attention that builds upon self-worth we seek out validation as an attempt to acquire approval. Who we acquire approval from is a factor that can destroy our future. What if the doctor in the story prescribed meds to Gillian rather than taking inventory of how she was gifted? There is a huge chance that she would have never been discovered at all. Even worse, she would have never discovered her gifts, or like many of us, she could have inevitably fallen victim to beliefs that produce little to no impact at all.

We need to understand how important it is to commit our thoughts to growth. We are each able to explore our inner divinity to create as God created and as he enabled us to create. Our passions, desires, dreams, hopes, and livelihood requires a sense of meaning that is shaped by who we become. When you decide to embrace your gifts and talents, you attract the competencies that will allow you to thrive.

Identity is more than a label, it is the embodiment of who you are and the purpose you were created to fulfill. Because of this lack of understanding, many of us hopelessly drift through life with no specific focus or aim. **The reason most people are unfulfilled is because they find comfort in pursuing *everything* except what they were called here to do**.

> The reason most people are unfulfilled is because they find comfort in pursuing *everything* except what they were called here to do.

Growing up I was challenged with a troubling perception of reality. Almost every example of humanity was modeled by someone who was incarcerated, addicted to drugs, gang affiliated, or involved in crime. As a result, I modeled beliefs and behaviors that weren't conducive to success or a positive identity. Two of my siblings paid severely. One of my brothers died at the age of eighteen, while the other is now serving forty years in prison. Criminal activity, dysfunctional behaviors, and other forms of destruction were normal to us. We were unaware that we were living a life and existence that was contrary to the plan God had for us. Living a mediocre life was never in God's plan for our lives, it was just a belief we subjected ourselves to.

William Barclay stated, "There are two great days in a person's life, the first great day is when a person is born, the second great day is when a person discovers why." If I were to add a third day equally important as the first two great days, it would be the day a person realizes who they were called to become. Who you are called to become is your compass. Your future self is anticipating that you walk in greatness and abolish mediocrity.

Every person on earth is destined to find their true selves, but many don't whole-heartedly seek it. The only thing that stands between us and God's abundance is the dysfunction and disconnection of the two. Although we all have distinct qualities that make us unique we also have an ugly truth that is attempting to devour who we are, and that in itself is dysfunction.

Key Principles:

- We are all uniquely created and have the capability to do great tings
- Our belief systems govern our state of identity
- Rites of passage is a vital component to identity
- We are defined by our experiences, core beliefs, and the memories that mold us
- Where there is no real sense of identity your purpose will suffer.

Pillar three: Dysfunction

Identity theft doesn't just happen when someone steals your identity, it's when you allow people and circumstances to rob you of who God called you to become.

How kind of dysfunction is operating in your life?

Do you sometimes feel you don't measure up or that you won't reach your dreams? If so, I totally understand. As a kid, I remember the overwhelming feeling of inadequacy. Especially during holidays, they were the hardest for me. My two brothers' fathers would pick them up and keep them for weeks. While they were having fun bonding and building relationships with their families, I stayed home watching my mother struggle to make ends meet. I complained to my mother. I asked her why my father wouldn't pick me up. The resentfulness she felt, compelled her to say, "He doesn't care about us."

That response was ingrained in me like a plank in the eye. I hated my father with everything in me. I cursed him and wished he died every time I saw my mother cry, stress, break down, or experience misfortune. At the same time, I also had a deep longing to be accepted. I wanted what my brothers had with their fathers. This created an insecurity that turned me into a people pleaser. I had a fear of letting others down and I had to acquire approval from others to escape the feeling of being alone. Can you relate? If so, how?

I met my father when I was twelve. The long-awaited hero that I couldn't wait to meet was seriously promiscuous and abusive. On the first birthday we shared together, he left me with a woman I didn't know. Every weekend that we were supposed to be together, it was pretty much the same. I was left with a new stranger. When I complained, he retaliated with a deep rage. Often times, I went to school with bruises, whip wounds from extension cords, and worse. Teachers wanted to report it, but I was so afraid I convinced them otherwise. The first time I tried calling my mother he choked me with phone until I passed out. His wife watched in fear. Sometimes this even happened in front of friends. I remember he picked me up in the air with his bare hands at a birthday party. It was the most humiliating moment of my life. Even though it's a distant memory the anguish still boils in my soul today.

These events began to shape who I thought I was. I was a petrified kid who despised authority. It felt like every time I gained any confidence or thought I could be great at something my father destroyed it. The pain, anger, and resentments I felt carried on in every area of my life. For a time, it defined who I was, and it was a form of identity theft. **Identity theft isn't just when someone steals your identity, but it's also the things in life you allow to rob you of your God-given talents and your destiny**.

There is an important tool in business called an S.W.O.T. analysis. This analysis evaluates the most important factors of a business. By evaluating *strengths, weaknesses, opportunities and threats*, it allows a person to acquire an overview of how this business or idea can distinguish itself among other variables. Let's take a moment to create our own S.W.O.T analysis of self.

Your strengths are what makes you unique. We spoke about Gillian who was a dance extraordinaire. Though we may be gifted, we still have to master our pursuits and those things that set us apart. Your weaknesses could be your flaws, we all have them. Even Jesus probably had funky feet. Come on now! He walked everywhere in sandals, and no one every stopped to think about hygiene? I had to throw that in there, c'mon it was funny! On a serious note, weaknesses could include procrastination, being indecisive, lacking clarity on your vision, having poor behaviors, or just flat out terrible etiquette. The goal is to build awareness around these factors. Understanding there are opportunities is how we can grow. I'll elaborate on this in the next section, but as you saw in the story with Biko, society thrived when the inhabitants pursued their calling. An area that I want to focus on in this section is threats.

Identity is the thermostat that regulates everything in our lives. It's the narrative within your belief system that dictates your worth. There is a thermometer or inner dialogue that dictates your wellbeing. It tells you several things, how much money you will make, the quality of your love life, how educated you will become what type of people you will be involved with, etc... So, let me ask you a few questions:

What are some factors that drive your sense of identity?

If the story that you been living indicates you aren't worthy of success, your life decisions will reflect this. If you were like me raised to believe you were inadequate, your mindset will reflect that. Every fragment of your perception will become heavily indulged in how you perceive yourself and others.

Like the story of Biko and Gillian we are often forced to succumb to certain realities that challenge the beliefs we have about ourselves. Sometimes it's the behaviors we tend to ignore that is preventing us from growing into who God desires. Sometimes it's the burden of pain and trauma in our past or present. Often times its fear, validation, worry or insecurities that rob us of who we are called to become. These are all examples of identity theft.

It's a natural tendency to place a title, subject, or categorization and to identify something. Most often these identifications come with certain classifications and characteristics that define the nature of that subject. For instance, growing up I went to the schools that classified students as "at-risk." The feeling of being "at-risk" carried a stigma and it meant we were "disadvantaged." It was societies' way of saying we were most likely to become failures.

The events in my life were shaped by my perception of self when I was young. Interesting enough by the age of 16, I was featured on Scared Straight, a show about juvenile delinquents who were on a path to prison. After being placed in a juvenile detention center, and having run away from home several times, I fell victim to drug abuse and witnessed the murder of a best friend during an armed robbery. From birth, I was placed in a challenging environment that was out of my control. Many people weren't defined by the conditions of their circumstances, but rather the impressions of their self-belief. We become what we internalize. Naturally I behaved as if I was "at-risk," because I believed I was "at-risk."

> *We can't control past victimization, which is what happened to us. We can control victimhood, how we respond to what happened to us. This is how we are ultimately defined.*

We all have a desire to fulfill the ideal perception of who we feel we are. It's not only human nature, but it's a reflection of our psychology. The danger occurs when we lack awareness of the internal and external motivation that guides the dialogue of our blueprint. When your blueprint is built on a foundation of dysfunction, your life will be a path of self-sabotaging behaviors. Let's take the concept of validation as an example.

Seeking validation from the wrong individuals can cause stigmas that some people don't overcome. The need to seek approval is often driven by ego, insecurities, or lack of confidence in oneself. Take the story of Gillian. She didn't blend into the social norm of the school. Although she was very talented her mother and the teacher misdiagnosed her. Yet when Gillian joined the dance school she was able to advance and even build a strong network with children who modeled her aspirations.

If you conform to everything around you in an attempt to feel validated, your self-worth is automatically diminished. This is the same with fear, insecurities and every other form of identity theft. Validation is for the most part, dangerous, but can also be a great motivator which we'll discuss in the mentorship section.

For this reason, you must define who you want to become and fight at all cost to achieve this ideal perception of yourself. Secondly, take inventory of your uniqueness. Where are you gifted, what is your talent, hobbies, interest? What skills can you develop to create more value for others. Third, what dysfunctions are robbing you from moving forward? Is there any pain, trauma, or other behaviors that are coming between you and your future self? We will begin to dissect that soon.

If we are bound by fear we will never experience greatness. If we are bound by validation we will become victims of rejection. Insecurities expose what you believe about yourself. The only way to disrupt these barriers is to first acknowledge they exist.

If we are honest, the perception of our own self-worth and self-value is what drives the narrative of our identity. In the bible, Moses was given the calling by God to lead the Israelites out of slavery, yet he *felt* disqualified based on his speech impediment. Just like some of us, we tend to define ourselves based on flaws or stereotypes society places on us. Remember, I was labeled an "at-risk" student. Disadvantaged doesn't mean disqualified. In fact, it means the opposite. It means there is an advantageous opportunity to acquire a greater sense of awareness. In the bible David recognized Goliath lacked character but depending on who you ask, David would have been considered "at-risk."

If you don't define your own worth everyone else will put their price tag on you. Evaluate the behaviors, prejudices, and stigmas that are getting in your way of you being great.

1. Have you ever discounted yourself and walked away from a better opportunity based on a flaw that you presumed you had?

2. What type of identity thefts are you allowing to rob you of becoming all you are called to become?

Identity thefts impact all areas of our lives, from financial health to spiritual and physical health. Without this sense of awareness, we render ourselves incapable of flourishing.

I have created a list of identity thieves that have robbed me in the past. Do any of these identity thieves resonate with you?

Comparison
The need to measure up with others

It is a natural tendency, an internal mechanism that views others as a benchmark. The problem is it causes us to view ourselves as inferior or superior to others. The reality is God equips people in different ways, and while we compare ourselves to others we will always fall short because God designed you to be you.

Conformity

Conformity is the need to suppress who you really are to fit in with others. This includes not using your gifts, talents or even your personality due to operating out of the norm. By suppressing what is inside of you, you are killing a sense of your identity.

Fear

Nothing robs individuals from pursuing their purpose like the fear of failure or fear of rejection or of the unknown. Imagine how powerful you would become if you weren't captive to this concept.

What type of life is fear robbing you of?

Count the cost of what you are losing. Write down a list of all of your great aspirations. Write "fear" next to them. As long as fear rules over you, it owns every dream you aspire to receive.

Dwelling on Past Mistakes

Have you ever noticed that people who are stuck in the past tend to live life like they are already defeated? They either talk about the good ole days or they talk about the mistakes they made, both of which they have no control over. The difference between those who are living and those who are building legacies is, legacy builders are visionaries who focus on what is ahead.

Key Principles

> ➢ Identity theft isn't just when someone steals your identity, but it's also the things in life you allow to rob you of your greatest potential.

- Everyone has strengths and weaknesses, opportunities for growth and identity thefts.
- Recognizing flaws such as insecurities build awareness.
- The perception of our own self-worth and self-value is what drives the narrative of our identity.

Fourth Pillar- Dissect

What beliefs, behaviors, and associations do you have to exchange in order to step into a greater version of yourself? In life, there are many things we have to let go of. In this section, we will begin to dissect these factors. Three major areas include:

- Beliefs
  - Leave behind beliefs that prevent you from evolving
- Behaviors
  - Challenge behaviors that limit your growth
- Associations
  - Evaluate and hang around individuals that challenge your growth

When faced with challenging circumstances we tend to flee our environments rather than evolving from within to overcome a condition. This is what happened to me in the 11th grade. It was in the month of May, on the last day of school. All I could think about was celebrating one of the most remarkable influences of my life, Arthur Wilson.

Arthur was my supervisor and mentor. He was one of the first people that reached out to try to help me and my best friend learn the value of hard work, ethic and character. He was kind, loving, and supportive to everyone in the community, but he also loved to *floss* (look flashy). He had nice clothes, a nice-looking car, and overall looked very successful.

I am reminded of the last time I saw him, Arthur picked me up for work, excitement was written all of his face. His wife was pregnant and due to give birth later in the day. His plan was to pick me and my best friend up, work the evening shift and go see his wife give birth to their baby girl after we were done for the day. His plan didn't include the store being robbed, or that he would end up as the victim.

As our work shift ended, we threw out the trash. One employee decided to stay behind while rejecting a car ride home. We waved good bye and hopped in the car to head to the hospital. As we were getting ready to drive away a masked gun man (one that we knew very well) pulled out a gun requesting money. Of course, we didn't have any money, but an employee told others that we had a night stash that we would be taking to the bank. The information was wrong. The gunman shot Arthur and killed him right in front of me and my best friend and ran away.

We were in panic--- we called the police and waited for them to come. All we could do at that point was watch Arthur die in our arms. We didn't know what else we could do. While Arthur was dying, his daughter was being born in the hospital. Imagine two teenagers seeing someone they loved dearly be shot and killed. It was the most disturbing thing I had ever faced. Even worse, this murder happened only a few months after the murder of my uncle. My mother had witnessed his murder. When I graduated high school the first thing I wanted to do was get away, leave. I thought if I could get away from my dad, the environment, and all the drama I would be better off. The first available option was the military. I left quick and in a hurry.

What I didn't realize was that I brought more than my baggage along with me. I had all of my clothes in my sea bag, but I had all of the past pain, turmoil, stress, anxiety and depression that rested still inside of me. Unfortunately, these factors played a role in these efforts to get away. I had no respect for authority. I hadn't managed my anger. And even when I moved around to different states and countries, I took my toxic beliefs with me everywhere I went.

Dissect Mediocre Beliefs

What story are you unknowingly defining yourself by? I come from a background that lives by the blame game. We blamed the "hood" for poverty, we blamed the government for social injustice, we blamed the economy for low pay wages, and of course, we blamed fathers for broken relationships. Sometimes my grandmother blamed the black cat that crossed the street for her check being short. Although the bible says, "With God all things are possible," somehow, we have a belief system that stripped us of the empowerment we are supposed to experience.

Does your belief system empower you to become greater or does it limit the capacity of your achievements? Are you giving in to excuses that prevent you from excelling in life?

My top excuses were, "my father wasn't in my life, so I'm broken, I don't have time to do such and such, I can't stay faithful to one woman, or I don't fit in with that group so…. you fill in the blank. We have all had to use excuses to get through. Staying confined within these types of beliefs meant I was not worthy of being healed, educated, accepted, compensated, and loved. To sum it all up in one word, I didn't feel "whole." I have heard people say things such as:

- I am late or never on time, that's just who I am
- I am loud and have poor etiquette, that's just who I am
- I will always be single, that's just who I am
- I am broke and poor that's just who I am
- I can't be faithful to one person that's just who I am
- I can't change this career, job field etc., that's just who I am

How can you grow or evolve if you give into the excuses that keep you stifled? Who defined these types of standards for your life?

As you begin to grow and mature do you ever question the beliefs that contributed to the person you are today? Even things like superstitions. My mother had this rule that we couldn't split the pole while walking in public. This meant if you walked past a pole, both people had to walk on the same side of the pole. We weren't allowed to open an umbrella in the house, and we were told if we broke a mirror in the house we would suffer seven years of bad luck. Can you believe that? Seven years of bad luck? I vividly remember accidentally breaking a mirror, and anxiety setting in as I began counting the days that this awful curse would be over. My grandmother taught my mother these beliefs and she learned this from her great-grand mother. As absurd as this sounds, this is some of the same logic that governs who we are.

When God created us, He desired for us to live the best versions of ourselves. By living the best versions of ourselves it empowers us to make the greatest impacts we can. That's a pretty impressive exchange for being created right? Every creator hopes that what he or she creates will provide value to the world. However, many of us are products of single-family homes and we grew up in toxic environments or were even raised to accept the influences that have resulted in adverse reactions. Those environmental influences created catastrophic damages that we are often unaware of.

A broken self-image leads to a broken life. No matter how you attempt to mold something that is broken, unless it is repaired it won't function as it was initially intended. Seeing a bird that can't fly because its wings are clipped would call into question what happened. We recognize the uniqueness of a bird for its ability to fly. This should be the same for us as well. The more awareness we have about ourselves, the more we have the ability to step into the next level of ourselves.

There is one issue, we tend to lack mindfulness or a sense of clarity in the present defaults that impacts our state of growth and being. Our minds are conditioned to become susceptible to certain influences rather we are conscious or not. This is even more evident in the social media age of viral videos. Children and adults watch viral videos and emulate actions regardless of how dysfunctional the outcome is.

Most often we emulate actions of those we trust rather they are deemed worthy or not. These actions transpire from our belief system which contributes to our behaviors. Our modeled beliefs are so deeply rooted in us that we aren't aware of them until they are challenged. If you tell me your pet peeve, I can tell you what you value. Your emotions are tied to the things you believe. From here we can gather what type of information is conditioned within our mindsets.

Expectations, beliefs, and behaviors are all tied to who we "feel" we are. The result of these outcomes either hinder us from growth of keep us in failure. For instance, self-sabotaging beliefs will cause you to flee any opportunity. As an example, it's like getting a great paying job but showing up late every day. Some people believe being late is a part of who they are. They lack time consciousness. Being late is a part of their belief system, therefore the result contributes to a behavior which all translates to a poor sense of identity.

How many of us date people and we see all the red flags, but continue dating them anyway? How many of us have poor eating habits to the point of destroying our health, but we continue to eat badly? How many people settle for jobs that limit their potential? I am guilty of all of the above! It is hard to admit, that in many cases I was the red flag! As you move towards actions that contradict or go against your limiting beliefs and behaviors it "feels" terribly uncomfortable.

A few years ago, I learned about "cognitive dissonance[4]." Let's say you bought a computer that came with software programs to download into it. The programs you have available are pain, trauma and misfortune. You have a friend over to your house, and they try to access your hard drive and they are looking for joy, peace, and fulfillment. The computer will reject any response in regards to this request. Why? Well, because the files you are trying to access isn't in the database. The neurons (cells) in our brain function the same way. We are molded by our own beliefs that are created from memories stored in our hard drive.

Anything that goes against these beliefs become severely uncomfortable. It's similar to being addictive to sugar or caffeine. Breaking the addiction would cause a disturbance. To overcome, we have to be educated about the physiology of stress hormones.

Since the perceptions created in our minds define our realities, anything that goes against your beliefs exposes the way you think. This evaluation builds upon what makes you feel like *you*. With this information we can "dissect" what beliefs are beneficial to moving forward and what beliefs are keeping us from moving ahead.

Emotional damage from enduring child abuse, and witnessing domestic abuse plays a role. Also, being conditioned to poor health, living in poverty bound by a scarcity mindset, created resistance to me accepting success. Breaking this cycle of dysfunction began with mental awareness. Without it we inevitably perpetuate generational cycles of conditioning. Since our brains are wired to protect us, we naturally settle into old comfortable programming. Even more dysfunctional, our stress

---

[4] Cognitive dissonance- the state of having inconsistent thoughts, beliefs, or attitudes, especially as relating to behavioral decisions and attitude change.

hormones will seek out certain psychological patterns to stimulate these conditions. It's like trying to avoid sugar. If your body is used to having sugar, it will create certain sensations such as the thought of getting a donut or cookie to scratch the "itch." If you grew up in toxicity and are prone to view it as normal than your mind will create this condition by seeking it out. This means by default we choose "mediocrity."

Psychology refers to the resistance within identity crisis as cognitive dissonance. According to this theory, people tend to model behaviors that are congruent or in alignment with their beliefs. When there are inconsistencies or resistance in these behaviors dissonance occurs. Being conditioned to a state of familiarity that doesn't challenge our growth results in a life of mediocrity.

Unresolved issues consume us from the very beginning. Insecurities, abuse, hatred, greed, depression, self- loathing, fear, doubt, worry, and anxiety create an elusive and deceptive perception of life and of ones' self is also a culprit. This eventually makes success difficult to attain. My goal is not to induce rumination where you solely focus on your flaws, but instead disclose your ability to manage toward evolution.

Identity can either shape you into a victor or victim but the two cannot coexist. Both of these two paradigms have differing natures that operate within their own. It is imperative that you pursue the identity that creates the greatest sense of authenticity. *This requires us to get clear on who we want to become.* When you define who you want to become recognize the resistance as programmed conditioning in your hard drive that has to be overturned to make room for the new.

Some have dreams they have abandoned, businesses that never started, books that haven't been read or written, collaborative business ventures that have been placed on hold. This means that fear is literally a yoke of bondage preventing capable people from receiving the legacy God has for them (identity theft). If you succumb to fear there is a chance that you'll never get to meet your real self. And, this is the goal of identity theft.

We are all impacted by many difficulties, and the internal conflicts that attempt to create barriers are always warring against us. The pain of unresolved *stuff* creates real barriers within the state of our consciousness that if not dealt with will become a shackle that limits your potential. If you have attempted to be better or to try something new, you can relate to the struggle of trying to identify with the alignment of your ideal self and the reality of where you are in life.

As promised, I want to get back to cognitive dissonance. It is the feeling you experience when you make decisions that are inconsistent with your beliefs such as cheating on your diet or thinking unrighteous when you know you shouldn't. It is the same thing an alcoholic experiences when facing the temptation of drinking alcohol. Something in the back of their mind says "I shouldn't be drinking anymore." Cognitive dissonance challenges a person's character. It is an excellent source of one's identity. When conflict occurs, you have three options:

You can adjust and reduce the dissonance by receiving the change and simply growing, you can have another thought and rationalize the dissonance, or you can fight the urge and change. For example, a person is unfaithful in their relationship. They may have a thought or an impulse that causes them to make the same mistake. They can either avoid the idea because a part of them doesn't want to go through the pain of hurting anyone else. They can have a second thought such as, 'I probably won't get caught.' Or they can use the cop out, 'Well, someone was unfaithful to me, so I have the right to be unfaithful.' These types of situations are in direct correlation to how one feels about themselves.

The lack of willpower is also another element of identity theft along with lack of self-discipline. The only way to reduce cognitive dissonance and end with a positive result is to challenge yourself. We must all challenge ourselves in weak areas in order to become the best version of ourselves. The resistance to growth that I felt in my life was a symptom of identity theft. Not having a clear vision of the greatness within me contributed to my cognitive dissonance. So, the question now becomes will *you* flee the growth you know you could experience? Will you wrestle with a constant state of cognitive dissonance or settle into behaviors that will keep you in bondage? Are you prepared to never experience what you were called to live out?

The image of wanting to become a leader without a reference point was a conflict. It's like wanting to become a great husband or wife without having dealt with the behaviors that were modeled in your youth. I had a desire to have a great family, but I struggled with anger and infidelity. Every relationship that I had before being delivered and saved by Jesus resulted in a trail of tears, and a path of brokenness. I found myself blaming every circumstance on someone else instead of the common dominator, me. In all honesty, this was a generational curse in my family.

Three generations grew up without fathers in my family. I grew up without a father, and so did my father. I have family that have spent more time in jail than in the free world. I have friends that have thrown their lives away due to substance abuse and even some that have lost their children in the system. If you were to take a look at these circumstances many of the behaviors that were learned were passed down through generations of *identity theft*. We have to dissect which beliefs and behaviors that are must destructive to our growth.

I'm the first in my family to graduate from college, to be married or have a marriage that has lasted over a decade. I am the first to own and operate a successful business, and to become a published author. As we evolve as the best versions of ourselves, we will be presented with new opportunities to make a greater impact on those around us. Our thoughts can positively or negatively affect generations to come. Be the first to do something great. This starts with a renewed mind. Now that we have discussed beliefs and behaviors, let's talk about associations.

Are you prepared to never experience what you were called to live out?

Key Principles

- When God created us, He desired for us to live out the best versions of ourselves to make the biggest impacts we could, for his glory
- Identity can either shape you into a victor or victim but the two cannot coexist
- People tend to model behaviors that are in alignment with their beliefs- when they don't resistance occurs- Cognitive Dissonance
- Awareness of this resistance is how you challenge programmed identity thefts

Dissect Associations

Being reluctant of the type of energies we allow in our realm is the reason many of us have become stuck in mediocrity. By associations, I'm not talking about the negative in-laws that you have to spend thanksgiving with or the annoying co-workers that only want to discuss drama and gossip, or the late-night boo thang that calls every once and a while to connect for relational purposes. I am talking about the people that you invest a great majority of your energy into.

Now, associations are important because as we stated in the last section we tend to model behaviors unconsciously that we are often unaware of. The basis of who we aspire to become is found in the characteristics we model and emulate. In the bible Jesus is a great example. In many references Jesus points out that he modeled after the Father. On many occasions the Father affirmed Jesus stating how pleased he was. The brilliance that is found in scripture is that Jesus always expressed the significance of intimacy. He built discipleship after Godly virtues, but also had an inner circle of three people (Peter, Andrew, and James).

Who do you have in your inner circle?
What type of attributes or values do they bring to your life?

_____

_____

There are many other scriptures that express the value of relationships. Iron sharpens iron, tell your sins to each other that you may be healed, we are the body with many parts, etc. If the creator of the universe was intentional about building relationships then relationships must be of some importance.

We discussed behaviors now we must become attentive to "how" certain people or groups influence certain actions. As an example:

- When I hang around old military friends, it triggers memories and we tend to drink too much alcohol.
- When I hang around certain family members I lose consciousness of time. This often causes me to be tired later on which impacts other areas of productivity.
- Some of my religious friends are overly judgmental and their beliefs cause me to become overcritical of how I view other people who don't think like me.
- Hanging around some of my friends that don't eat healthy causes me to be relaxed in my own health consciousness.
- When I hang around my friends who tend to be socially minded than business minded, they sometimes disregard my aspirations. This causes me to think in terms of complacency, rather than acting on what I value most.

Some may argue that I am easily influenced or lack self-discipline, but the goal in this section is to empower you to own your potential. By recognizing beliefs, behaviors and associations, you can acquire a sense of clarity in how you are being developed. It's important to note some people in your life don't care if you become successful. Ten, twenty or thirty years from now there will be people who wished they took actions on their dreams but didn't. I still have associates from high school who are in the same position they were when we graduated high school. They are playing dominoes at the same table, reciting the same old stories and have all, but forfeited all they aspired to achieve. This will always be the same. Your level of happiness is dependent upon how much you evolve. Please do yourself this courtesy and be mindful of how you allow associations to impact your future.

There are so many people living in opposition of what they were created to be. The conditions placed upon them serve to limit who they are. My grandmother and mother thought I would be dead by the age of twenty-one. Now, I stand here not only as an author, but as an educated one, to tell you and to show you that I followed these simple principles:

1. I defined what I wanted my life to look like.
2. I discovered my own uniqueness after taking inventory of my skills and talents.
3. I evaluated the dysfunctions that plagued my internal belief system.
4. I dissected the associations that translate into the desired individual I wanted to become.

We were all given the authority to step into greater versions of ourselves and to overcome the stigmas that tend to bind us. My goal is to help you acknowledge where you are and what you need to do to change it. There will always be opposition, let's dissect those things:

1. What are some negative thoughts you have about yourself?
2. What are some negative beliefs others have about you?
3. What are some behaviors that contradict your growth?
4. What are some influences that keep you stifled?

In this stage you should begin to think about who in your circle needs to be eliminated or moved out of the balcony. I am sure you may have heard, "your network is your net worth or "You are the sum of your five closest associates," or, "Show me your five closest friends, and I will show you your future." How about, "Misery Loves Company?" We have all heard those clichés and have even grown to love and recite them. Associations shape us in more ways than one. For this reason, it is vital that we take inventory of the people we allow in our lives.

There are four supreme truths about associations and how they impact identity:

1. We grasp a sense of who we are by modeled beliefs and behaviors.
2. A great deal of our learning occurs through observational learning and mimicking others.
3. Behaviors are tied to what we give our attention to.
4. Memory, motivation and often our actions are directed unconsciously.

Step into a growth atmosphere

Have you ever heard of the "crab in a barrel mentality?" This is a mentality that drags anyone in a group down if they try to advance. When a crab sees someone trying to get out of the barrel the group (or individual) pulls it back down. This mentality occurs often in *mediocre* groups. For this reason, you must learn to determine which group is most valuable to your season of development.

Do the people in your circle inspire you to do greater things or do they become threatened by your growth?

_____

_____

Are the people in your life providing direction or are they distracting you from your purpose?

Direction or Distraction

Have you ever used a GPS system believing in its guidance with full confidence and faith only to find out the directions it gave you was inaccurate? This has happened to me on multiple occasions. It's even worse when you are in a hurry during rush hour traffic with bumper to bumper traffic, next to a driver with poor driving etiquette. Sometimes I stop and think to myself why has this GPS taken me so far off the route I'm supposed to be on? I placed information in the GPS expecting to be led in the right direction, and was taken off course. This is how some of our relationships are.

Some individuals play instrumental roles in providing direction for your dreams while others do not. Make a list of those who are goal oriented, have vision, and the leadership you need. Make a list of those who are only involved for social reasons, they aren't always the best *directors* if they have no desire to go anywhere. How can you tell the difference? If you express to someone in your circle that you are thinking about giving up on a dream, goal, or idea, become attentive to their reaction. Most times the responses you get from those who don't fully support you sound like this:

• Man, it's about time you give up on that, it's not going anywhere
• That's cool, let's hang out and do something different!
• I understand, just go back to doing what you used to do!

If they respond with either of these comments or anything else that encourages mediocrity, they have not discovered their own self-identity and they are not ready to help you discover yours. Now, if they say something like:

• What did God say about that decision?

- Is there any way I can help?
- What other solutions can you come up with?
- Have you prayed about it yet?
- What is next, what do you need to do to make this happen?

Either of these responses or anything positive leading you to be who God called you to be is a que that you want to stay connected to them. They are wanting to see you win in a way that encourages your growth. They intend to provide direction, and they are leaders in the GPS field of instruction.

People who inspire you, will provide direction. People who are toxic will produce distractions. One group desire to see you win and won't let you settle, the other group is solely concerned with you only if it benefits their own agenda.

One group inspires from within and motivates to action by helping you produce the right results. You should connect with people because of what they represent and because of the impact they are making in your life and the lives of others. Toxic people enjoy getting attention to suit their own comfort and are even willing to over dramatize situations to deter you from your goals. Inspirational people don't get engulfed in gossip because they are goal oriented, while toxic people have no goals in mind, so they are *wandering generalities* (people who wander aimlessly with no goals or foresight).

I encourage you to join a mastermind group, a faith-based group or any other group that inspires. Having likeminded individuals that challenge you to think on new levels is imperative to breaking though mediocrity.

Every Jock Needs a Cheerleader

My biggest supporters are like cheerleaders. Who are the biggest supporters in your life right now? Show them appreciation. Cheerleaders are there when the chips are down and they show up when the team is winning. Cheerleaders show up when the super star is benched for fouling out and when the star is performing highlights. Cheer leaders not only wear the team jersey to show support for the mission, but they prepare the hearts of the crowd for the game. The role that cheerleaders play is very important, and it could make or break a team or individual.

The angels in heaven come to mind when I think of cheerleaders. Although God is incredible all by himself He created angels to worship. Worship "sets the atmosphere," and cheerleaders set the atmosphere and prepare the hearts of the crowd for a good game. Often the stars in the games are highly recognized, but the individuals that support behind the scenes rarely get any recognition. These are the kind of people that reinforce your sense of identity and impresses upon you to reach greater heights. These individuals don't sugar coat anything, and they aren't afraid to have serious conversations. They have one goal in mind --- to see you win.

Winners Circle & Mentorship

The most impressive individuals in your life will cultivate aspirations that already exist within you. This works by giving you a greater sense of identity. Many of us have an *unexplored star quality* living dormant, waiting to be awakened. Star quality can be awakened, this is what great associations do. Great people inspire you to acknowledge and embrace a higher version of yourself. Great people inspire you to reach new standards by enriching your quality of life. This enables you to purposefully examine unexplored levels of consciousness you may not have even been aware of.

What if you could leverage someone else's experience for your own benefit? Would you do it? What if someone who is more than twenty years older than you could give you all the insight necessary to direct you to your destination, your greatness? Would you listen to them?

Oprah Winfrey had Dr. Maya Angelou's wisdom to glean from for many years, Mark Zuckerberg was inspired by Steve Jobs, Dr. Martin Luther King, Jr. was mentee to Dr. Benjamin Mays, and Bill Gates was molded by Warren Buffett. Each of these great men and women were powerhouses already on a trajectory of greatness. Imagine already being "great" and having someone with impeccable skill and experience hand over a golden ticket to you. This is exactly what mentors are…winning lottery tickets. A mentor is a straight shooter, not a friend but a person who is primarily in your life to help you grow, to have the difficult conversations, and to assist in your transformation.

Mentorship doesn't have to be person to person, it comes in many forms, including consulting with leader in your industry to work with, seminars, a podcast or online references, or books. Some people have achieved enormous amounts of success and put it all in a book. Some have grossed millions of dollars, and placed all of their wisdom in a book to sell for twenty bucks or less.

When I first started my business, I had no idea what I was doing, I was frustrated. My mentors took me under their wing and developed me. They recognized competencies that needed to be improved and they also noticed the strengths I didn't realize I had. This is the environmental impact of mentors. This is what is so incredible about God, and certainly what you place in your mind is what you become. Maybe you don't know any millionaires, but one day you very well might know many of them. They are doing podcasts, seminars, and writing books as we speak! Some of the information has their emotions, philosophies, experiences, and environmental influences all over it. All it takes is one idea to be impressed upon you.

Acquiring experience and wisdom from others is the best education. Mentors have specific expertise and have already achieved what you are setting out to accomplish. They recognize the mental tenacity necessary to achieve goals. They have the resources to catapult or jump start your ideas.

Most mentors are aware of their duty to give back, and are most often willing to provide wisdom. They may be careful about who they mentor, and there are a couple of reasons for this. They feel entitled to a degree, to instill some or all of what they learned and in small ways, they want to ensure their own legacy. Mentorship is by far is one of the best exchanges known to mankind. If you ever wonder why two likes attract, there you have it. Being mindful of the people in your life indirectly or directly impacts every area of your life.

This section is meant to shed some light on how influences and associations impact identity. Let's discuss identity according to the word of God. Who else to give identity than God, the creator Himself.

Key Principles

- ➤ As social creatures we learn best through osmosis.
- ➤ The basis of who we aspire to become is found in the characteristics we model and emulate.
- ➤ The most impactful individuals in your life will help cultivate some of your talents and aspirations, giving you a greater sense of identity.
- ➤ Mentorship is by far is one of the incredible exchanges known to mankind.

Almighty Already: Explore God's divine origin of your identity

We finally arrive to our last section, "Almighty Already." There are two types of people in the world, those who let their environments define them and those who design themselves based on their aspirations. One side of the coin settles for mediocrity and the other side settles for nothing, but the best. Begin to think about who God is calling you to become.

Throughout history there is no denying that there is something internal within us all longing to connect with something greater than who we are. Whether through prayer, connecting socially online, or through travel--- our desire to connect stems from God's very own intimate nature. Scripture states that God is love, so our longing to express the illustration of this beauty stems from the mechanics of how God shaped us.

Manifestation of Greatness

You are the manifestation of Gods' glory. You indeed are the physical manifestation of greatness.

You are the manifestation of Gods' glory. You indeed are the physical manifestation of greatness. Lack of the divinity within us is the biggest form of identity theft ever! The natural origin of who God called us to be and to become leads us into greater aspects of ourselves. This happens when we listen and when we are led by God's anointed voice. When our steps are ordered by God we are in direct alignment with our calling. "Identity has so many layers of evolution, if you are planning to settle in life, why not settle for the best version of yourself?"

Godliness challenges every deficiency within us, by aligning our inadequacies with a supreme and divine notion of excellence. There is a problem though, as Dr. Joe Dispenza[5] said, "We don't see things as they are, we see things as *we* are." When this is true, pain, insecurities, regret, failure, and trauma etc. overshadows the abundance of beauty and the love we are capable of seeing for ourselves and others. For this very reason we have to be reborn. When we come from a past of misfortune, we expect nothing more from life than misfortune and what we have gotten in the past, or what we have seen in the past. And while this may be true for some, God calls us to leave behind anything that blinds us from the truth and our identity. We were all created to be great, because we are children of an incredible God.

Greatness is not something to be obtained but something to become. You don't have to pursue greatness because God already made you great. Instead you have to remove the impediments that tells you otherwise. For this reason, you are…"Almighty Already."

If you are like me, you didn't grow up with a healthy perspective of religion and spirituality. In fact, growing up many pastors of churches cast me out. One pastor even condemned me to hell during the funeral of my little brother for wearing ear rings to church. I was only twenty or twenty-one years of age. It was quite disturbing. I sat in the pew grieving with so much anguish over my brother's death and at the same time, the Pastors' sermon was about me going to hell! His exact words were, "There is no Heaven for a thug." This hurt so much but, I'm

---

[5] **Dr Joe Dispenza** is an international lecturer, researcher, corporate consultant, author, and educator who has been invited to speak in more than 33 countries on six continents. He teaches about Neuropsychology and how to rewire your brain and thought patterns to achieve optimal results.

grateful that someone saw some much more than pain when they looked at me.

I was in my senior year of high school when I had a divine intervention. At this point in my life I was kicked out of the house. There was a really violent altercation between my father and me. In a violent outrage he tried to hit my sister while she was having an asthma attack. I stepped between the two to defend her when my father punched me in the face and dragged me down to the floor. At this age I was able to defend myself. Although my step mother agreed with the actions I took she felt it best that I no longer live under their roof. Therefore, I got emancipated at the age of seventeen.

After weeks of sleeping on couches of multiple friends' homes, I got a job, and found an apartment with a roommate. They probably weren't the best influences because we had drugs going in and out the home but at least I had peace. The following week my clique at school came up with a bet for the Valentine's Day party. The bet was we had to ask someone totally opposite of who we were (personality, characteristics, etc.) to the party and get them to go. There was this girl in one of my classes who was extremely sharp, well put together, and basically "nerdy." She was totally the opposite of what most would consider a "hoodlum" or someone like me who was a "little rough around the edges." For weeks I invited her to the Valentine's Day party and she declined. Eventually she agreed to go on one condition, I had to meet her mother. I agreed.

Her mother's name was Patricia Jarrett. She was a woman of power, virtue, strength, and intelligence, unlike anyone I had ever met in my life. She had short black curly hair, dark brown skin, and a smile that could light up the heavens. As I approached the car to meet her she reached out to give me a hug and said, "Son, I've been waiting to meet you my whole life." The comment struck me in such an awkward way. No one had ever approached me with so much enthusiasm and passion. She asked me to get in the front seat of the car so we could talk.

As I got into the car it felt like much more than an invitation to the Valentine's Day party. She proceeded to unravel a lot of the misconceptions I had about myself. You see, Pat was the first African American retired police officer in Oklahoma. She spent her whole career involved with children that had similar stories like mine. The difference is, while everyone else degraded, disregarded and lost hope for me, this woman saw so much more in me. She began to tell me that I was intelligent, had a big heart but no platform to display it. She stated that I needed to be in a healthy environment in order to thrive. She told me I would go to college and achieve great things and help so many people. I remember laughing because I was blinded by so much dysfunction I honestly thought, "Yeah okay lady, (I wanted whatever she was smoking). The truth is, for some crazy reason I sort of believed her.

We began to meet for weeks and she became a mentor to me. After about a month she told me she could no longer let me stay in the same condition and invited to move in with her. She said, "You are no longer just a date for the Valentine's Day party, you are my son." She fought hard to help me understand this power she saw in me. At times I just didn't understand it. I didn't feel worthy of this type of love and grace. One of my friends got in trouble with guns and she bailed us out with no charges on our records. There are many more stories that of her having my back, but I'd rather not incriminate myself. All I can say is it was a grace I can't explain.

In the end, there were two outcomes I wanted for myself. First, I wanted to become whoever this woman saw me as. I didn't know this person could exist. And secondly, I wanted to align this person with the type of love she had for me. She loved me a lot because she knew I was deserving of higher standards than I settled for. This is when the journey changed drastically for me.

Who Does God Say You Are?

While Adam and Eve were in the Garden of Eden, Satan attacked their very foundation. It wasn't the ripeness of the fruit that persuaded them to go against God's will but the fact that Eve wanted something she thought she lacked. In the bible, Satan told Eve that eating the fruit would make her like "God," but the bible says God made "man and woman" after his own image and likeness. This image is the premier focus of this chapter.

Are we celestial beings molded from dirt, fragments of the universe created from star dust, or animals with software updates? This is a question that has piqued the interest of historians, theologians and scientists for ages. The mechanics of how we are configured magnifies how awesome and intricate God truly is, think about it:

- We are unique in the mechanics of our biology. We are equipped with the ability to evolve, heal, and reproduce.
- We are spiritual beings with the ability to transcend and manifest different levels of consciousness.
- We are relational and able to connect through chemistry, culture, and community.
- We are complex in the structure of our anatomy with the instinctual human nature of survival.
- Our minds are electrochemical, meaning both electrical and chemical properties.
- Feelings, emotions, and thoughts create energy with the use of neurons that produce motion.

We are so much more than tissue, billions of cells, DNA, muscles and skin tones. God shaped us with greatness in mind. Though we are fearfully and wonderfully made, each of us have great potential that is often left unfulfilled.

There are dimensions of human consciousness that I'm most impressed with in relation to identity. Most profound is the human trinity in terms of the mind, body, and soul. Each layer of our makeup is just as vital as the other, but most often we invest heavily in our bodies and neglect our minds. While some spend heavily on their bodies, they tend to ignore their spirit. Since we are made in the image of God, with God being a spirit, it's crucial that we invest time in the spiritual essence of who we are so that we prosper in all areas of life. Taking a holistic approach to identity redefines every aspect of our being.

God's original purpose was to create leaders that would shock the world. In the Bible, the children of God had such valor placed upon them that the world was impressed to join the family. Leaders such as Daniel found favor in God's eyes and succeeded in everything he did. Joseph was a dreamer who faced tragedy, but overcame it, due to the purpose and will God placed on his life. In the book of Acts, people were so astonished by the love, joy, and peace that resonated from the hearts of those who loved God, people began to sell everything they owned to pursue His nature. In many ways, having character is important, but having compassion is powerful. You must have compassion for others, and you must most definitely have compassion for yourself. Everyone has some form of dysfunction, but when they align themselves with the will of God their lives became a reflection of His favor. This concept helped me birth the idea of *Almighty Already*. Everyone God used became a new version of themselves. They became the version God had already known they were. Each of us are fully equipped to do great things in life. Many of us are geniuses with undiscovered talents, qualities, and abilities just waiting to find our platforms. *It's not just who we are that gives us identity, but whose we are that molds our identity.*

You are called to be Kingdom

"There is no inferiority about the man that God made, the only deficiency in us is what we put into ourselves."

In the bible, God specifically said we are made in His Image and after His likeness. Any narrative that you are living that contradicts this word strips you of the purpose He created you to live out. Understanding the wisdom of God invites us into "essence" of our own worth. With God's wisdom we are able to find our purpose and ultimately abolish mediocrity.

Our foundation is exemplified in how we live. When God calls us into His kingdom, royalty was embedded and woven through the fabrics of our being. Your ways of thinking should be adjusted to a higher climate. The way we walk, talk, and operate should inspire others to see and feel the presence of God. Since God is a king and He is our father, everything that is of royalty and everything he considers great is available to us. Therefore, God draws our hearts, minds and souls unto him to mold our dialogue into His presence. God is also called "love," so the nature of his love should cause us to know love and to become love.

When we operate from a conscious state of love for ourselves and others it destroys the fundamental beliefs associated with inadequacy. We no longer become victims to the irrationality of ignorance that states we are born to be weak, powerless, and hopeless. <u>The power of this perception abolishes mediocrity.</u>

We should operate from a conscious state filled with love for ourselves and others. Not doing that counters positive fundamental beliefs that are associated with inadequacy. We are not meant to be victims of irrationality, nor slaves to ignorance--- born to be weak, powerless, and hopeless. This power abolishes mediocrity.

Since God is the creator, He is the source of all living organisms. For this reason, we are viewed as one with Him. Each one of us play an intricate role within the dynamics of each other's pursuits. This contradicts common destructive practices of division. When we are divided it interrupts the progression of our calling. God views us as a body that functions to optimally maximize our potential while we are unified. The body represents many organs that function together to maximize performance. Each of us have spiritual gifts that complement each other. We as one person are only part of the equation. When we are fragmented as an individual, we are more than likely divided as a whole. If we are disconnected from spiritual nourishment, God cannot fully communicate the nature of God to us. This is required to maintain and create growth in our identity and calling. There is a small voice in each of us that seeks to guide us to truth. That voice speaks to us quietly about we are and what we should be doing. As in the story of Gillian, the small voice was fighting to express her destiny. Denying the essence of who we are restricts God from moving freely through us. When this occurs, we are led into brokenness, division and a foundation built on identity crisis.

As a father that desires nothing but the best for his children, Gods' desire is to see us all as royalty, and yes this is a journey each of has to take. This includes examining the way we think, the way we control or steward our emotions, bodies, mind and soul. Our perception of identity is essential to God, that's why he continually shapes us for his purpose. Our presence should cause others to question their own passion and reasons for existing. Can you identify individuals who have committed to having marriages that thrive? This defines loyalty and love. Who are these leaders who would rather die in jail, or face scrutiny than to compromise their character or beliefs? This is the definition of integrity. These are the same characteristics of an unfailing God.

The beauty in God's approach is that He strategically identifies what is in us based on the nature of what's in Him. The cracks placed in us by tragedy, defect, or our parents will be filled with his wisdom, compassion, and unfailing love for us. Because we are made in His image, by default we are automatically unified with him through DNA. While the world tries to identify us as "damaged goods," God sees a broken vessel that was created for his spirit to flow through. This perspective identifies something inadequate or altered, *damaged or broken*, while God sees something that is operating out of the scope of its identity or what it was created for. God specifically associates his creation with purpose.

Because God is a Holy God, he aspires to remove sin from our lives so we can see Him in us, and so we can see much clearer. It is interesting though that our sin and brokenness didn't disqualify God's chosen leaders in the bible, and it doesn't disqualify us. We will still build legacies. When we come from a state of brokenness we often eventually recognize the value of grace and mercy. Grace is a free gift that can't be bought, so Gods love is a love that is unparalleled to any variation of love that man can offer.

This is the unique premise of this book, because everyone is under construction and for us to grow God will challenge us with new extremes. God may advise you go to a different place than where you grew up. Abram was challenged to be a father of many nations like Abraham who shifted from Abram to Abraham. God led the Israelites out of Egypt to strip the slave and victim mentality from their beliefs. He may have to separate you from your environment to allow you to envision purpose.

You may be asking, "What does this have to do with identity?" The best way to understand creations is to evaluate the Creator. God desires to make all things new.

He wishes to give us all a new nature that promotes and creates abundance, peace, righteousness, and grace. He also wants us to live a life that allows us to prosper in the unique abilities he gifted us with.

Can you imagine what the world would be like if each person knew how God individually wired them and engineered them with gifts, talents, and abilities? The possibilities would be impressive. What if God placed you in the best position to maximize the potential within you? The more you realize your purpose, the more passion you'll have to follow your pursuits. You would want to serve out of admiration just like those who are genuinely in love. The emotion that flows from love is remarkable. When you are in love with something or someone, your beliefs shift to improve the ways you can become more efficient. When you love yourself you treat yourself better, you invest more time in yourself. You can forgive, heal, and provide grace in areas that are limiting you. This is why we need to understand what we are called here to do, and only God can give us that knowledge.

I once heard someone say, "There is no inferiority about the man that God made, the only deficiency in us is what we put into ourselves." What God made was perfect. Your upbringing, background, downfalls, or other's opinions don't matter near as much as the way God sees you. While you may feel inadequate, he calls you a "Mighty Hero."

The bible says God is love. He loves with such a deep, passionate, and resilient love that when individuals come in contact with him, they are healed. I have seen blessings flow even when we are in a state of brokenness. God is a provider. I have witnessed my life change during moments of despair. God is a way maker. When all hell breaks loose, and we are lost, I have seen God restore peace. Our Lord is a peace maker.

To God, we are perceived as a worthy treasure.

I grew up with a victim mentality, I was heartbroken, and depressed. It was difficult to come to grips who God had intended me to be. When I was finally in tune with God, things changed, because I no longer had to seek validation from others.

Don't wait for the world to crown what God said is already royalty! God not only created us, He knew we would experience unfortunate circumstances, and therefore He was prepared to impart grace with intentions of shaping us for his divine purpose. Everyone has their fair share of struggles, but God gives us the ability to be made new (2 Corinthians 5:17), we are then provided with insight into the nature of God.

Connecting with God strengthens our spirit

Just like the physical body has to exercise to stay fit, our souls remain fit through the nourishment of God's presence and His word. Prayer elevates a level of consciousness that creates awareness of the conditions within us and around us. The more we connect with God, the more we come into the knowledge of our own purpose. Just like any other relationship, the more time we connect with specific individuals, the more they become a part of our well-being. This works the same with God. We discussed the impact of internalizing things, as well as how beliefs contribute to identity. God the father is a spiritual being and the orchestrator of our lives. Our thoughts and beliefs will direct our lives.

The spirit is broken down into three sections: matter, neurons and consciousness. God requires us to meditate on his word day and night. This is the process of reprogramming false beliefs that have conditioned in the subconscious mind. The Holy Bible isn't just material with words in it. The written scriptures are alive and contains a spiritual essence created to connect us with the divine nature of our Holy Father. As we seek out other means to fill this void, we usually discover temporary fixes, because nothing can fill such a vast space. Gods' will for our lives causes us to elevate towards new heights because of the constant renewing of our hearts and minds. What God seeks to do is to renew our hearts, mind and souls by reshaping who we are based on his principles. The more we tune in to His purpose, the more passion we develop towards fulfilling why we are here in the first place.

One day I had to keep it real with myself and actually acknowledge the fact that the dreams I aspired to achieve wouldn't occur for the person I had become. I had to adjust the vision I saw for myself to identify the pathway I needed to head toward. Sometimes it isn't the beliefs we have about ourselves that is limiting where we want to go, but the visuals that we allow to define us along the way. What areas in your life need to be reevaluated? How have you planned out your path in a way that doesn't quite align with God's plan? Review these key principles for enlightenment:

Key Principles:
- ➤ God blessed us with a celestial divinity that longs to connect with a greater purpose.
- ➤ God wants us to live a life that allows us to prosper in the unique abilities He gifted us with.
- ➤ God seeks to renew our hearts, mind and souls by reshaping who we are, based on his precepts.
- ➤ By adopting the identity God instilled in us, we can fully walk in our calling.

Exercise:
We are plagued with negative thoughts about ourselves, this is your time to recondition your mindset by aligning the perception you have of yourself with the word of God. Your words were meant for edification. I encourage you to write out affirmations to affirm the

excellence God placed in you. Words have power. Create daily affirmations about how victorious you are through. Speak life with the authority God birthed in you!

Try these:

I am alive. I am loyal. I am love. I am faithful. I am satisfied. I am gifted. My home is blessed. I am a new creature. I am a mighty hero. I am loved by God. I am kingdom-minded. I am still and at peace. I am a resourceful friend. I am a child of the Lord. I have power over my enemies. I am filled with the Holy Spirit. I am the righteousness of God. I am bound by the love of God. I am precious in the sight of God. I am healed emotionally and mentally. No weapon formed against me shall prosper. I am dwelling in the secret place of the most-high. I am submitted to God and the devil flees from me. I am heir of God. I am full of life with good health. I am strong and of good courage for God is with me. I have refuge in the Lord. I am covered by the blood. I am debt free and do not owe anyone anything but love. I am full of the spirit of wisdom and the revelation of God. I am strong in God might with the whole armor of God on. I have prosperity. I am blessed and rich in the Lord. I am abundant and fruitful.

If you don't have a strong vision for your life you will spend most of your time stuck in the past. Legacies are created from a projected vision that allows us to anticipate what is to come.

What type of life do you envision for yourself?

_____

_____

_____

CHAPTER TWO: THE BARRIERS OF A BROKEN VISION

Second Barrier to Mediocrity: Lack of Vision

Vision is evidence that anything is possible. Mediocrity is the result of us abandoning a worthy pursuit.

The second barrier to mediocrity is a lack of vision. Dr. Wayne Dyer said, "You need to learn how to create a match between what you desire in your life, and what thoughts or vibrational energy you're choosing to attract those desires." With that in mind, know that nothing conceived in the physical world was created without first being imagined in someone's mind. From fidget spinners to technological advances that allow us to orbit foreign galaxies, the only limitations we have, are the ones we place on ourselves. Vision translates into beauty by taking the story we can't see for ourselves and turning it into reality.

In the beginning of the bible, in Genesis, God said let there be light and spoke the universe into existence. We were given the greatest cues about what it means to have vision. Regardless of our circumstances we have the ability to create through vision. Our lives are void without a vision. The reason why you and I are breathing is because the infinite intelligence of the universe desires much more from us. We often have much more to give. The narrative that you give to this story will define your vision.

Take time to examine everything around you, understand that every tangible object came from a manifested thought. Before anything was ever created, someone conceived it with intention. When you feel stuck in your job, relationships, finances, or life, I want you to take a step back. Close your eyes and imagine a life free of these perceived barricades. The power of visualization allows us to evaluate every perception we have created about our own reality. As we draw closer to our purpose, this often requires us to leave something behind. It forces us to align ourselves with a greater sense of purpose. This alignment begins a process of removing that which has caused stagnation, conditioned behavior and negative beliefs.

In chapter one, we broke down the barriers of identity, now we will step into the barriers of vision. For much of your life someone has placed limiting thoughts on you about what you are capable of achieving. They did that by placing your value in a box plagued by limited capabilities. Today I want you to call forth your vision as God proclaimed it to be. Think about and believe when God proclaimed He is faithful to complete every good work He began in you. Today I want you to imagine every chain that has hindered your progress, broken! I want you to envision every negative thought, as destroyed. Walk in victory and replace those defeating thoughts with empowering thoughts.

Vision is the ability to see beyond the typical conditions that bound many to mediocrity. Today, at this point in your life, the victor in you desperately needs to aspire to new heights. Nothing paralyzes the human species like the lack of imagination. It's our imagination that propels us into our own divine uniqueness. In this chapter, I want you to channel your inner child. I want to reawaken the part of you that isn't afraid to dream and believe in greater things. What do you see for yourself, for your family, for your community, your future? Do you have a vision or a strong *why* that drives your life into purpose?

Do you have a defined outcome that you want for your life? Your family? Your ministry?

The four questions I want to keep in the forefront of your mind to challenge you to overcome mediocrity:

Who are you?
What is your purpose?
What is your mission?
What drives you to achieve a desired outcome?

Without a vision of greater, we hopelessly live in the past.

One of my greatest heroes growing up was my uncle. He was athletic, intelligent and had a great love for art. As a child, I admired how he would draw fancy pictures and drop them off during rough times in our youth. He played dominoes with my brothers and I, and made a habit of dropping off money to every once and a while. My uncle was a sharp business acumen who was hired into leadership positions in every job he worked at. While in his youth, women were attracted to him, colleges scouted him, he was the "golden child" of the family.

One summer, something very disturbing occurred. My grandmother dated a man that took advantage of my uncle and performed explicit acts. It literally stripped him of his dignity. The whole family knew something happened to him, but no one did anything about it. In fact, not only did the family know about the incident, but they made a public spectacle of him, by teasing him. The pain must have really affected my uncle because he dropped everything. He walked away from his scholarships, quit sports, and became heavily involved in drugs and alcohol. He went from being a genius with a bright and aspiring future to a broken vessel that had given up on everything he loved. My uncle was one of the first people to discuss higher education. The pain that he felt became the defining aspect of who he was. This shifted the belief system of what could have been possible for his life.

One day, my uncle decided to go and score some drugs while he was supposed to be babysitting us. The guys he left us with molested me and my brother. My family was too drunk and high to even care. It happened a few other times before it became apparent that something had to be done. This type of behavior trickled down causing traumatic damages. The conditioned reactions of drug and alcohol abuse became normalized.

The painful memories and trauma associated with these events shaped who we believed we were was based on conditioning and situational trauma. Because we most often recycle the traumatic experiences in our brains, they have the tendency to mold us.

As I began to heal, I came to the realization, that there are people who shape their lives based on events that happened to them. Then there are people who design their life based on visions of achieving much more for themselves and others. Adopting a vision for your life, will create a force that pulls you towards something greater.

Benefits of Having a Vision

Vision is proof that anything is possible. Mediocrity is the result of abandoning a worthy pursuit. Vision is one of the most underdeveloped abilities that God gave us. Since we are conditioned to take the path of less resistance we usually settle in life. We settle for any old mediocre job, mediocre relationship and even mediocre belief systems. We lack clarity in the factors that stifle our imaginations. We are aware of the power that clear direction gives us, but we often lack clarity about where we want to go in our pursuit. Lack of clarity binds many to mediocrity.

Visionaries are born from captivated visions that draw them into innovative practices. Legacies are created from vision. Vision inspires us to be greater, to go farther, and to elevate. Without it, we are doomed to mediocrity. Visionaries solve the world's greatest problems. Among the many attributes that visionaries have, their ability to *master their obsessions* is the most admired. Many times, these obsessions come with a steep price. Visionaries are ridiculed for being hopeless dreamers, innovative thinkers who challenge flawed methodologies. The result of achieving their worthwhile pursuits have consistently revolutionized society. Martin Luther King Jr. is an exemplification of this truth. The "I have a dream" speech occurred at the height of his life and career. It exhibited his purpose and calling. This speech challenged a system of patterns and beliefs. It also challenged the reality of times, racism, and it also challenged the vision that people had for their lives.

Among the many creators that shifted society, the story of George Washington Carver expresses just how powerful understanding your life's purpose is. Born into slavery in January of 1864, George Washington Carver[6], was not expected to one day be a proclaimed genius. His life story includes having been born into slavery, during the Civil War, kidnapped, yet he knew he was born to lead. His parents Mary and Giles were slaves to owner Moses Carver. Shortly after his birth, clan members raided the field he worked in, kidnapping the young Carver, his mother, and sister. This caused an uproar among the slave owners, Moses hired an agent to retrieve them. The detective began immediately seeking to locate the mother, child and sister. Sometime after the search the child was located in Kentucky. Unable to locate the mother and sister they were proclaimed deceased along with Carver's father

---

[6] George Washington Carver was an amazing inventor that overcame through the power of vision and passion of his gifts. Though he lived under difficult circumstances and extreme conditions of slavery and racism he was able to overcome his environment and contribute a great deal to society.

who was murdered on a nearby plantation. With both parents deceased, Moses and his wife Sarah assumed parental duties to raise young Carver.

Since it was difficult for Blacks to attain education, the Carvers taught George how to read and write. Sarah, Moses wife noticed Carver's extreme interest in education, but it was his natural curiosity that sparked his obsession to venture outdoors. While outdoors he was able to freely investigate the many wonders that fascinated him. Being a keen observer to nature he began to collect different plants, flowers and other attractive specimens to evaluate and analyze.

The young genius had a knack for knowledge, a great hunger and ingenuity for music, art, and agriculture. Since his intellect piqued beyond what the Carvers could teach him, they encouraged him to further his education through travel. The difficulty of acquiring an education was challenge he was willing to overcome.

There were no schools nearby that would accept *enslaved Negro children,* so at the age of twelve, Carver traveled throughout the city of Kansas to find a school. With racism being such an extreme factor in the South, Carver faced much scrutiny, abuse, and rejection. While searching for education he decided to work jobs to make a living. Eventually he found a school ten miles away and obtained his high school diploma at Minneapolis High School in Minneapolis, Kansas.

After graduation Carver was accepted into Highland College in Highland, Kansas. He furthered his studies by conducting small biological experiments at home from the specimens he gathered. Although his brilliance proceeded his reputation the school reconsidered his admittance once they found out he was colored. He decided to keep working and focus on his passion. A friend told him about a college he was attended, although it was an Art school, Carver became excited because art was his second love. Shortly after the conversation Carver joined his colleague and began studying art.

In 1890 he began his studies in music and art at Simpson College in Iowa. The instructors were highly impressed with the passion George exemplified in his sketches of botanical samples. The natural aptitude was so evident in his drawings that they encouraged him to apply for botany school to pursue his passion. He was then accepted into Iowa State College to purse his major in Botany, and eventually achieved a graduate degree in Botany.

After graduating from Iowa State, Booker T Washington hired Carver to teach at Tuskegee. It was here that his life's most important aspirations began to show. Carver's extensive research as an agriculture leader and knowledge in chemistry opened doors for him to *expand and flourish*. Though there were limited resources, his ability to create thrived and his perspective to shape and mold continued to manifest. This was the creative nature he nurtured through art. Art expanded his inner genius by giving him a creative space to take an idea, mold and shape it as a sculptor by modifying clay. He became deeply immersed in the details, opening his mind to possible solutions that weren't yet discovered in his industry. By studying the unique diversities of chemical compounds, he was able to thoroughly examine the nature of expanding specific resources with limited commodities. He recognized art was a tool. He could take one thing and imagine many different purposes from a single specimen. The ability to create and manifest with concentrated effort broke through the limitations of miniscule resources. This allowed him to achieve his God ordained calling. All of his students were inspired and this transcended from Carver's leadership making Tuskegee one of the most sought-after schools in education.

Carver believed we have a divine duty to steward the earth with the utmost care. Due to this belief he developed extensive contributions to revitalize crops that led to economic stabilization in the South. He discovered crop rotation, a technique that helped farmers boost productivity. He helped revitalize the earth's natural composition of soil through nitrogen and other efforts to repair damaged soil which helped to harvest better crops. As an agricultural chemist he developed hundreds of uses for sweet potatoes including postage stamp glue, vinegar, rubber ink, and molasses. He also took the same approach with peanuts creating more than three hundred different alternative uses from milk, soap, and oil. With southern farmers struggling to overcome the barrier of cotton manufacturing due to climate, Carvers vision changed everything. Due to his exemplary work, leaders such Theodore Roosevelt and Mahatma Gandhi sought advice on improving agriculture. Carver had become an iconic figure around the world.

Developing a vision for your life allows you to become intentional about the things that matter most in your life. This is proof that living out the greatest version of ourselves empowers us to build monumental visions. Carver faced indifference, racism and rejection, but God's purpose for his life empowered him to do so much more. He pushed passed adversity, grew more intentional with his efforts and even revolutionized the South, culture, and race. This allows us to see setbacks as part of the journey. The best way to have the life you want is to create it. *If you don't create the vision you want for your life, you become a victim to the conditions of your life*. **Most often we can't control the situations we were born into, but we can choose to define them. When creativity comes alive, victimization dies. When you cast your vision, your gifts have room to expand.**

What is that one thing that calls you to pursue far more than you have ever imagined?

Key Principles and Points

- ➤ Nothing conceived in the physical world was created without first being imagined in someone's mind.
- ➤ Vision is proof that anything is possible.
- ➤ Among the many attributes that visionaries have that make them unique is the ability to *master their obsessions.*
- ➤ Vision allowed Carver to cultivate limited resources and catapult it with the power of vision.
- ➤ Living out the greatest version of ourselves empowers us to build monumental visions.

Direct the Narrative of Your Story

Those who achieve much in life do so because they execute vision that brings clarity. Sometimes this clarity can be questioned. Think about situations such as choosing a career or going back to school. Even those things require the assistance of the "Holy Spirit" or the "small voice" to govern our direction in alignment with the purpose God created us for. There is often a disillusionment (disconnect) from passion that is created when we fail to align ourselves with God's plan for our lives. Failing is an epidemic that occurs when we seek out conventional means for success. The result of living this way strips us of the passion we were created to harness for greater works. When we live a life counterintuitive to our desired vision, we suppress the most authentic identity that longs to be revealed. A greater sense of our identity is found in the vision we pursue for our lives. The quicker you align yourself with the vision, the faster you attract the competencies, purpose, and joy you were created to experience. Unfortunately for those who don't find this truth, they will forever be subjected to mediocrity.

When a person becomes clear on their purpose, it rewires the circuitry of their beliefs. Clarity provokes a mental stimulation that demands fruition from the universe. This is why people that have endured hardships and misfortune rise from impossible situations and soar to incredible heights. The art and science of achievement is found through vision. Vision defies all laws of logic. People have used vision as an instinctual tool for survival.

Carver developed a growth mindset, set his heart on the things he loved, and served others with passion and enthusiasm. He stayed on a course of action that enabled him to expound on his gifts. This truth was also seen in the story of Victor Frankl. In his book, "Mans search for meaning," he noted that Holocaust survivors projected a narrative that something greater in the future awaited their presence. This narrative allowed them to survive the hell they were living in.

This power of motivation also worked for athlete and motivational speaker Aron Ralston[7]. While rock climbing he became stuck in a canyon when a large rock fell on his arm. He attempted chipping away at the rock in order to free himself. Unable to release himself the rock he collapsed from fatigue after five days of being stuck. At this point all of his food was consumed, he had drunk his own urine to survive and began recording a video for anyone that found him dead. Unable to get himself out of the predicament he fell asleep and began dreaming. In his dream, he saw himself as a father. Though only a figment of his imagination, he saw himself picking his son up from school, celebrating birthday parties, and taking his son to the park to have fun. The joy, passion, and expression fueled the instinctual need to survive. He woke up, broke the ligaments in his arm and cut through his arm with a dull pocket knife. This false narrative fueled a super human motivation through the psychology of human belonging. Visualization saved his life. This is a pretty grim story, but we often sell ourselves short by not harnessing the value of vision.

Vision has many benefits. Of the many benefits to note is that it drives the narrative of our stories. Since the goal is to go from "living to legacy," anything that drives us into purpose is imperative. Vision creates a sense of becoming new, because it produces growth. It challenges any and all programmed beliefs that are maintained in our unconscious minds. Once you align your ideal life with your vision you will have successfully been rewired. Every

---

[7] Aron Ralston uses a vision of a little boy (his future son) to combat the pain he was feeling to free himself from a wedged rock. This vision of a false narrative fueled his enthusiasm to break free to get to his family. This was an internal survival mechanism that aspired him to survive.

limitation that has defined you will be reconditioned to conform to that which God said is so.

We most often admire leaders and their influence because of their views and perspectives. Vision shapes perspective and provokes action. The bible says, "Faith without action is dead." Vision takes our minds out of default mode through the effort of emotional stimulation. We become motivated by what gives us a sense of passion and fulfillment. Vision is what distinguishes the mediocre from *super-achievers*. What would life look like if every hero or role model failed to execute their vision? They would no longer be considered the heroes you admired. People are truly defined by the actions they take in life.

Though racism was a challenging factor for Carver, he was able to adopt an identity that defined his era. Eventually his vision helped alter a common belief which allowed him to become a major contributor to society. Same with Henry Ford, he cultivated an aspiring vision that shifted the auto industry. Ford was extremely gifted in imagining parts assembled together to create mobility. Albert Einstein could formulate the calculation for the relativity theory before it could even be proven in space. Nikole Tesla, like Henry Ford was another inventor that was extremely talented. He channeled his mental concentration to create a desired outcome. He too shifted our society due with his imaginative thoughts that were manifested. These creators solved major problems, regardless of adversity and speculation from others. Creativity is how one creates freedom.

Vision creates methods for your gifts to be used, which brings you in touch with the impact you are designed to make. This requires us to define our uniqueness and to define the distinct achievements we long to fulfill. If you don't feel skilled enough to build upon your vision now, create a projected resume that you would like to achieve in the future. If there isn't a vision that pulls you towards your future you'll find yourself stuck in the past. Evolution is the result of an achieved vision.

I won't sugar coat as if vison is a fantasy. It isn't a filter on Snapchat, Instagram, or Facebook. Vision is a lie detector test that exposes the internal scars and behaviors we try to hide. It is human nature to pursue that which is comfortable. We are naturally wired and even addicted to homeostasis (normal health state of condition outside of fight or flight). Vision on the other hand is something we can't throw a filter on. It takes consistent effort to have the ideal life you desire for yourself. Vision calls our bluff when we attempt to lie as if all is well. It is similar to a mirror or bench mark that exposes the intimate most innate parts of who we are. We often overlook and ignore these parts of ourselves. When we develop a vision, it exposes the behaviors, feelings, thoughts and emotions that are preventing us from moving forward.

It's important to note how vision impacts mindset. Our minds are set to a default mode that performs like an algorithm. Throughout the day we subconsciously search for patterns to make life as easy as possible and any of our choices become automated. The routine order in which we brush our teeth, get dressed in the morning, the route we take each day, when we eat are all conditioned automations. These are actions you can perform with the least amount of energy. Vision gives you ownership to take over your mindset and to become intentional about what you want for your life.

When you start to pursue higher visions that call you to greatness you'll hear negativity such as, "Why are you even trying this or what do you hope to gain from this pursuit?" You will begin to hear all the negative self-talk designed to get you to give up. This is negative self-belief that has been programmed into your subconscious mind that needs to be disposed of to create the ideal life. In ongoing chapters well further discuss bio-hacking your mindset.

Develop an achievement-oriented vision through the power of intentionality

There are few things in life you shouldn't be passive about, and vision is one. We have discussed the problems that occur with vision and the benefits of vision now let's discuss an action plan for developing clarity. As long as you have a vision that propels you towards a defined outcome, you have the ability that governs your narrative. Manifestation is the ability to bring the desired vision to fruition. Jesus himself spoke about this in Mark 11:23 (NIV) when he said, "Truly I tell you if anyone says to this mountain, go, throw yourself into the sea, and do not doubt in their heart but believes that what they say will happen, it will be done for them." This spiritual principle lets us know that we have the ability to shape certain perspectives based on our desired outcome. In most cases, we don't believe we can achieve the outcome we so desire, so we don't pursue it, this is why Jesus spoke of "Doubt in the heart.

This also references how we can channel our emotions to shift our belief system. When we desire certain things and place expectations upon ourselves, our brain-wave energy harnesses power into those thoughts. Remember that vibrational energy is fed by our expectations. This calls for our emotions and thoughts to be on the same wave length. A double-minded man will have to overcome doubt. Doubt is a resonating conscious belief that will restrain you from being immersed in your vision. This is why vision is crucial. It fuels your emotions and feeds your faith to achieve the desired result. This requires us to have a renewed mind.

Do not overwhelm yourself, it's okay to start with incremental or small steps in order to bring your vision to life. Have you ever created a bucket list? A bucket list is nothing more than a list of experiences you would like to fulfill in this lifetime. Just like a house or a building in need of infrastructure which provides efficient support, your vision needs a blueprint. The more specific, the better the outcome. A bucket list illuminates what's most valuable and important, many times the items on a bucket list risk never being explored.

I am reminded of a story about a man who became bored with his mundane life, uninterested by the monotonous routine of his daily obligations, he fell into a deep depression. He went to the doctor and told him of his long list of medical concerns. After conducting a thorough examination, the doctor found no health issues. In complete denial, the patient refused the doctor's prognosis. He exclaimed loudly, "Doc something is severely wrong." After objecting the doctor's observation, the doctor decided to tell him he had a rare disease that left him with only sixty days to live.

The doctor then asked the man to write out a bucket list of all of the things he wanted to achieve before he died. Alarmed by this minuscule time he had left the man pulled out a sheet of paper and immediately began writing all the things he wanted to complete within his remaining time. On the sheet of paper, he wrote down all the incredible things he wanted to do with his time.

He decided he would take the bucket list and write stories about it along the way as a means of remembering the final days and passing it along. All the things he wanted to do, he did. Leading up to his last few days of life with only a couple of weeks left, he decided to visit the doctor to update him on his condition. Upon seeing the doctor, he reported, "Doc, I feel amazing, my energy levels have increased tremendously, my wife and I have explored an amazing journey, and my story is inspiring others to pursue their dreams as well.

The bucket list idea was genius. Vision has been flowing like never before. My marriage is amazing, and I met the family that I haven't seen in my life. I learned to fly a plane, I published a children's book that is doing well and have now replaced my income and I can travel full time with my wife. I wish I would have done this years ago, I have achieved more in these few weeks than my whole life." The doctor responded, "Well that's great because now you can have a lifetime to continue your efforts." Surprised at the nonchalant response, the doctor told the man that he was perfectly fine and no longer had any sicknesses. They both laughed and the man was excited about this news.

Skills, competencies, joy, passion, were all present when the man identified with what he wanted. Vision even created a sense of urgency.

How many of us live as if we have an unlimited amount of time left? Vision allowed this man to create fulfillment and impact. A lot could happen within two months of continuous, concentrated effort dedicated to your vision. If you really focused on your bucket list, what do you think you could achieve in two months?

There's nothing wrong with being specific about what is most important to you. The people that are most successful in life aren't successful because they are crazy rich, have all the glitz and glamour like Janet Jackson or Jennifer Lopez. They are successful because they have narrowed down their vision to identify what they want out of life. They have also developed the drive to go after it, they have resilience and grit. Most people don't know how to identify the ideal life they would like to pursue. This was a critical issue for me.

Answer the following questions to develop your own action plan. After meditating on these questions and writing out the answers in a journal, you will be enlightening in ways you never have been before.

Action Plan questions:

1. What do you want to be known for?
2. What gives you a sense of fulfillment?
3. If you were given a blank check to quit your job and live out your dream for 3 months what would you do?
4. If failure wasn't an objective what career path would you pursue?
5. What type of success do you see yourself creating?
6. What type of hobbies stir passion and enthusiasm for you?
7. What mark do you want to leave on Earth?
8. Plan out the next 10-15 moves ahead in your desired plan of execution. What system of order do you need to cultivate to grow into your next level of life?

The bible reminds us that, "We have not, because we ask not," so asking with the expectation of certainty is a universal law and a biblical principle. Ask God to lead you and be led by His wisdom, there you will find guidance. You can ask God any questions regarding your future: Is education in the cards for me? If so, what should my education focus be? What type of relationships do you want me to have? Should I relocate? What career should I pursue?

One of the guys I mentored asked, "Why does clarity matter? For all we know life may not even be real, and this could all be a figment of our imagination." My response was, "Exactly!" A majority of the experiences we are living out is but a reflection of our own consciousness. Rather in the conscious state or within our subconscious mind our perception of our reality is often directed by our thoughts. In fact, imagination and vision has taken human beings and placed them on the moon. That outlandish idea became a physical representation of a desired manifestation because it was *specific*.

Manifestation

Manifestation is the *mental* action of taking an intangible thought, action, or behavior and bringing it to fruition. It is the taking of matter in the conscious state of being or imagination, using concentrated effort to bring about a defined cause, purpose, or result. The problem with many of us is that we don't concentrate enough on the things that require the most attention.

You can manifest your desire to be a great father, mother, son or daughter. You can manifest the desire to become a great leader. If you don't like your family, no problem--- manifest yourself a new family! Not exactly, but...you get my point! You can manifest the desire to acquire riches, to lose weight, shed body fat, have a successful relationship, be an author, artist, engineer, director, etc. You can even manifest the accumulation of generational wealth to pass down something of great value for generations to come, just like George Washington Carver did.

Just for clarity, this is not the positive thinking shenanigans you may have heard of in the past, such as prosperity gospel. Nothing, in reality, will ever manifest itself that wasn't once cultivated in your mind. There are parts of your brain that can't tell reality from fiction, therefore you have to give your mind the right ingredients to create a desired outcome. Manifestation doesn't discriminate, it doesn't care if you are black, white, purple, brown, or orange. It doesn't care if you are broke, poor, or rich. All human beings can become better versions of themselves.

The difference between lower income impoverished areas and the suburbs is the ideal perception created between the two. Growing up in the hood for me depicted an unfortunate livelihood plagued by drugs, stress, and lack of success and opportunities. The imagery of the suburbs reflected the opposite. If you define yourself based on an environment, you will grow to think and believe a certain way. You will be led to identify yourself with the disenfranchisement you experienced growing up.

This was my problem, destructive beliefs defined the vision I thought possible for myself. This is why some people are afraid to step outside of their comfort zone and try new things. Achieving greatness requires us to leave a part of ourselves behind in order to elevate to levels God designed for our lives.

The culture I was raised in dictated my sense of vision, it was an environment of limited beliefs. Your experiences can make you feel that because you come from brokenness, you deserve just brokenness. Vision, on the other hand, always seizes to make you elevate. I am grateful for the people in my life such as my wife and mentors. Along the way they consistently challenged my perception of reality.

There is joy to be seen, a passion that unheard of, and a grand vision that has yet to be explored. You MUST be attentive and intentional about the things that God will create through you and in you. You haven't laughed your best laugh, wrote your best song, dreamed your best dream, or lived your best life if you haven't explored vision.

Using vision to manifest your desires is a birth right given by God. The bible states, "For nothing is impossible with God." If God gives you the vision and guides your steps, then why should your faith be limited? There are usually three elements related to vision that challenge most individuals:

1. People don't believe they can attain the things that would give them purpose and meaning.
2. They haven't been able to pinpoint God's will for their life.
3. They don't perceive themselves as being worthy of the responsibility greatness requires.

Any of these three things speak directly to *identity crisis*. Some will still argue that others have advantages such as coming from a family of wealth, receiving government funding or some form of corporate backing. What about financial resources that can create significant advantages?

You have to keep in mind that it doesn't matter how much money you have in the bank. In fact, when you pay more attention to the advantage others have, it takes your eyes off God, and what He has for you. Focusing on others places your perspective on things that do not matter.

What you focus on manifests in your reality. Even if the perception you have is skewed by your life experiences, God can change that. Someone with a vision has reconstructed parks in ghettos where drugs used to be sold. Sight has even broken limiting beliefs off of individuals like myself. From heartache to broken promises, vision has been a testament in my own healing, and is literally the reason my marriage thrives.

Suspend your disbelief --- and move forward as if creating a television show as it is occurring, crafting a dream with no limits. What dream would you pursue if you knew you couldn't fail? From now on, go at it with this type of mindset. Interestingly enough, when we watch TV most of us are aware that we are watching some form of entertainment fabricated with fictional characters. Nowadays some of what we watch is "scripted." We tend to suspend any disbelief associated with what we are viewing, and allow our imaginations to roam freely.

Even when the programming is fake we allow our subconscious minds to become *impressionable* by suspending any disbeliefs associated with the content, because the subconscious mind can't tell the difference. We then develop mental stimulation that draws upon our emotions to make it seem real.

Can you do this with your vision? Can you allow yourself to become fully submerged in your idea to the point that your disbelief is suspended as if you're watching a movie? Creating the story as it is occurring? Allow your subconscious mind to process vital information as visuals and this will allow you to dictate the frequency you want to project in your pursuits. If you can use this same approach for your vision, then you can rewire conditioned beliefs on a higher scale.

Key Principles
> Vision conditions your thoughts, emotions and energy.
> Start small with your vision by creating a bucket list.
> Vision breaks the barriers of a conditioned state of programming that is keeping us stagnant.
> Manifestation is the "mental" action of taking an intangible thought, action, or behavior and bringing it to fruition.

Paint the Picture

Without steps, procedures, or strategies in place we are missing what God has in store for us. God is all about the process and most often we are not. The journey is 80% of the mission and completing the quest is only 20%. On the journey we will most likely develop faith, wisdom, insight, character, knowledge, and understanding. The trip refines and shapes us into who God designed us to become. At some point we should all arrive at a state of gratitude---this is the highest form of consciousness.

Know what you love and what brings you passion; Be specific about what you want; Write it down and meditate on it daily; Mark the time of achievement; Study over your vision while you work your job; Work your dream as well as your job; Never compromise your values or your integrity.

Avoid the uncertainty felt by deciding to take *the leap!*

Steve Harvey is known for encouraging people to just, "take the leap*.*" Well, often we are afraid of the leap because of the *uncertainty*. Vision allows you to put a *face* to the uncertainty by developing the perception and the outcome you desire and expect. Sometimes we have to take risks when it comes to landing in your destiny. As a person who felt stuck in dead-end jobs, I had to learn to make calculated risks.

Developing a vision for your life allows you to identify the what-ifs, carefully. When I wanted to open my own business, I painted every detail of what it would look like to have an office and began carefully researching to appease my imagination. It is either stepping out or remain a hopeless dreamer. As Les Brown said, some people fight change as if the difference would be worse than their current circumstances. If God gives you an out, go for it and don't look back.

The Far-Reaching Benefits of Vision

A person without goals risks being known for their unrecognized potential rather than their gifts and talents. The state of mediocrity is a stage in which one has decided to no longer strive, but to explore aimlessly without a destination. This is what many of us are doing when we live our lives on repeat. Victor Frankl said it best, "Between stimulus and response there is a space. In that space is our power to choose our response. In our response lies our growth and our freedom." Ultimately, vision produces freedom---and this is where we get to reap the benefits of having a vision.

I listened to the great Dr. Myles Monroe give a sermon on vision. He stated that he didn't date while in college because he wanted to stay pure and devoted to the calling God had on his life. Due to his vision, drugs and alcohol were not an option, because protecting his mind was important. His vision dictated the standard of relationships he needed. His goal was to stay grounded and to develop wisdom and insight. Vision secured his integrity and character while providing boundaries for his pursuits. The sight made way for him to make an impact in and around him for God's glory.

Imagination allows us to create distinct visual images necessary in identifying what our destination looks like. Ever heard the saying you miss 100% of the shots you don't take? The only target you can arrive at is the vision your mind conceives.

Consult God's Wisdom

Realize God's will for your life begins with provision, security, favor, purpose, and love. We are endowed with the opportunity to make a difference using what God equipped us with. This helps us to understand that nothing God opens us up to will harm us, but it is for our growth. When you embrace this mindset, it makes the uncertain so much more promising and so much more, certain. God *prewired* us for this journey. Let me repeat this, so you can reread it, and get it down in your soul, God prewired us for this journey. Not just you, not just me, but us! He designed us, knowing we could and many of us would overcome any trials or distractions.

Take inventory of your current perception and think long term

Walt Disney was known for his tenacious imagination and often cited for his ability to effectively communicate his vision. What was thought of as a "Fairytale" is now the most visited vacation resorts in the world. Although he isn't alive to witness the impact of Disney World, his vision lives on as a gift that brings the best experiences to those who visit the theme park. Big dreamers create legacies that are remembered long after they are gone and often result in creating value for increasing the quality of life.

Regardless of your age you can identify that life is all about experiences. From moment to moment what will define you is what happens during your existence and how you respond to it. Individuals who live a true legacy are those who have disciplined themselves to make the most out of each second they are given. Each second presents an opportunity to bring out whatever you want it to. Just like God gives us gifts, he gives us time, and time is definitely a gift. We have no control over the past, but the future is all yours. Build your vision with the end in mind, sometimes the true gift is the legacy you leave behind.

Visualization is powerful because it challenges behaviors, mindsets, and factors that contradict ideal pathways. Visualization constructs neuro-circuitry (patterns of neurons in the mind) to focus the mind to the most progressive pathway. **Over 90% of our choices are driven by unconscious habits that lead to mediocrity**. In order to elevate your life, you have to elevate the narrative guiding your life. In other words, govern yourselves according to the vision that challenges your state of evolution to combat stagnancy.

Key Principles

- ➤ Paint the most desirable outcome for your life to avoid the feeling of uncertainty.
- ➤ Having vision provides boundaries to obtain the life you seek to achieve.
- ➤ God has fully equipped you to fulfill the vision He placed in your heart.
- ➤ Visualization is powerful. It challenges behaviors, mindsets, and factors that contradict the ideal pathway to progress that makes our lives worthwhile.

CHAPTER THREE–THE BARRIERS OF A BROKEN MINDSET

Third Barrier to Mediocrity: Poor Mindset Management

*The success that you experience
is dependent upon how well you
manage the mindsets that
govern your life.*

We have successfully discussed identity and how it drives our narratives. We have spoken about the importance of having a vision and how vision provides direction, provokes action, and shifts perspectives. Now, we will talk one of the most importance aspects of our journey---mindsets.

One of the world's leading photo corporations Kodak[8] had digital technology far before anyone else. Once known as a giant with a strong hold on the market due to its strategic business model, many never thought such an economic shift would occur. The refusal to alter their mission statement impacted their future. While everyone else moved to digital processing, Kodak went bankrupt. This is what happens when we fail to adopt a growth

---

[8] Kodak had digital technology in 1976. The business model for the company allowed them to create profit from production of film. They could have shifted the business model to create digital tools such as cameras, etc. but refused to innovate. Due to the major shift the company filed for bankruptcy.

mindset. My goal is to challenge limited beliefs and anything that causes you to become stagnant.

We are often our own worst enemies. For many, the beliefs we have is the only thing standing in the way of greatness. We are insecure creatures made in God's image. We *should* eat healthy, but we prefer junk food. We make commitments that we don't fulfill. We notice all the red flags in relationships, but we settle for dysfunction. We subconsciously reject any form of growth, yet we desire to improve. Internal beliefs guide who we are. The same mind able to meet our wildest imaginations is also one that can creates barriers.

If there is a challenge to confront in order to overcome mediocrity, it is self. The tendency to be lazy causes us to prolong the things we value most. The desire to procrastinate delays the success we are able to achieve.

Lack of self-discipline and restraint can lead to sexual compulsion. The unhealthy relationship we have for food causes us to indulge in toxins that shorten our lifespan. These toxins affect our moods, behaviors, and cognitive functioning. All of these factors are just as harmful as the negative thought patterns we subject ourselves to. The success that we create comes from how well we manage the mindsets that direct our lives.

Abolish the Mindsets that keep you Captive

I had a victim mentality and blamed everyone else for my problems. I blamed my father for the abuse. I blamed the system for my lack of advancement. I blamed the environment for the toxic setbacks in my life. Even when my checks were slim I blamed the government, taxes, and child support. The truth is I was born into scarcity and accepted poverty as normal. I was raised in poverty with minimal resources, therefore my psyche communicated that all I was destined for, was poverty. In the hood there aren't many jobs, so people steal, sell drugs, and participate in other illegal activities to provide for their families.

A study showed just 1% increase in the unemployment rate results in an estimated 37,000 deaths. For this very reason, it's imperative that you identify your purpose, because the building of your dream could save lives, literally.

Growing up, my brothers and I fought perpetually over small things. We fought over the Nintendo controller (which shows you my age), over who would use the bathroom first, over the tube of toothpaste, even over someone taking the last cookie or dessert. We were so affected by scarcity, our limited mindset produced unhealthy exchanges between us. I remember one year having my tennis shoes stolen. Nothing yells scarcity like someone taking tennis shoes off of someone's feet. These are circumstances created when one doesn't become intentional about adopting an abundant mindset. Scarcity will tell you to withhold from others, so you don't compromise your own personal resources. Insufficiency will cause you to be *stingy* and focused only on your own wellbeing. In this state, you risk the lack of understanding in how your actions impact everyone around you. Scarcity will cause your well to dry up faster than you can imagine. In this mindset, you aren't allowing the law of reciprocity to overflow with abundance.

The law of reciprocity works like this, when you open yourself up to help someone else, your hands are open to receive. Reciprocation comes as a result of being open to exchange. You become a pathway, a vessel in which God can pour into you. While you are intentionally giving, God is receiving the signal that you have more space for storage, and before you know it, you become kingdom-minded.

What if God had a scarcity mindset? There would be no such thing as abundance, and this would go against His identity. The same goes for us. We were created to innovate, to expand and to produce. In this same way, God requires us to care for ourselves and those in need. Allow

God to expand your mind by being a vessel. Scarcity creates coagulation. If a vessel gets a blood clot it kills the body, so does a scarcity mindset. To paint a better visual let me illustrate mindsets between the mice, elephant, and the lion.

The Mice, Elephant, and the Lion

In a scientific study with two groups of mice, one of the groups were placed in a small pool of water about two centimeters deep. The other set of mice was placed in frozen water. You can imagine one set of mice diving into the water splashing and having fun as if it were summer time and they were attending a pool party. The other mice were entirely demonized--- frozen bitter at the kneecaps and struggling while fighting to free themselves.

What do you think the results were for the two sets of mice after a period of time? After they were released, do you think they both went back to their original state of living? Nope, not at all. The mice that were happily swimming carried on as if nothing happened, while the other mice didn't move a muscle. Even after the mice were released they refused to move forward. This form of conditioning paralyzed them mentally. Just like the mice in the study, many of us have internalized false beliefs that have bound us to limited boundaries of achievement.

There are many factors that contributed to the mice not moving forward. In many cases its human nature to behave like the paralyzed mice. We often make promises we don't keep. We think of dreams we don't pursue. And though we aspire to change, motivation doesn't last very long at all. I've attended a lot of seminars, read lots of motivation books, created hundreds of vision boards, yet when I look at my life I often feel stuck in the same spot--- while everyone else is moving forward.

Socrates said, "The unexamined life is not worth living." Many of us are living in the matrix, plugged into a system that doesn't reflect the life we want to live. This matrix is providing us with thoughts we don't want to have, adopting beliefs contrary to our sense of achievement. It's like an elephant tied to a wooden stump as a child. When an elephant is only a baby the owner ties its leg to a rope and hammers a stump into the ground to prevent the baby elephant from wandering off. The strength of an elephant is unparalleled to any other animal, they are powerful. An elephant can lift over 700 pounds with its trunk alone, however an elephant is conditioned to believe that it can't remove a stump while it's young. Therefore, it doesn't fight the barrier, because it perceives it as impossible. Just like the mice in frozen water, their mindset has been conditioned to recall the circumstances that provided barriers and trauma in the first place.

If you were to analyze the beliefs that causes or have caused stagnation in your life what would they be? What is the stump in the ground that is hindering you from progress? For many of us its fear, pain, or historical trauma. We have to carefully monitor what beliefs are most effective to our development and what beliefs are most damaging to our growth. Once you align your beliefs with the identity God placed within you, you become like a lion. The lion is well known for its position in his habitat. It is not the strongest, most intelligent, or the tallest of animals in the kingdom, yet it holds prominent status in its habitat. A lion evokes fear because of its mentality and confidence. Other than its majestic appearance, a lion is just a large cat with a loud roar. It wakes up every single day with an innate intention to rule over every other animal within their habitat. The lion moves in a system of authority, and everything around this animal gives respect. Unlike, the *mice* and *elephant,* governed by a stagnant sense of belief, the lion knows it was created to rule.

Would you be surprised to know that an elephant is an animal that has the most self-awareness compared to other animals? It can even recognize itself in the mirror. Though it has this incredible advantage, there are still barriers that can prevent it from flourishing. This too is true for us. Take time to do some introspection or self-evaluation to understand and cultivate the ideal mindset to become more like a lion.

What type of belief system does a lion have? What imagery is a lion known for? First, it is known as the king of the jungle.

What belief system are you operating in? Are you like the mice, watching others excel while you wait for your turn? Are you like the elephant that is captive to limited beliefs? Are you like the lion who knows it was created to lead? The choice is yours! Resetting your mindset must be a priority. If you are not operating in an optimal state of mind your body will not produce the kind of results that place you at the top of your game. When we are grateful, joyful, passionate, fulfilled, and focused we can achieve everything we set out to do. At this level, our highest vibration is radiating with an energy that welcomes greater. On the contrary, when we are functioning as victims we are not in control of our lives. This cause us to be insecure, worrisome, depressed, indecisive, and fearful. We therefore become defensive, unfruitful and ineffective. Remember, God calls us royalty and expects us to walk in that title, to embrace the calling that was placed upon us. In fact, in the bible it clearly states that we are a royal priesthood and He calls us chosen.

Who contributed to your belief system?

One of the most troubling truths in regards to the elephant was lack of awareness in "who" contributed to its belief system. It's just like Adam and Eve when they were told by Satan to eat of the fruit in the garden. They were not confident in what God had given them or what God had told them. They already had access to everything they needed, but they wanted more. Destruction comes into play when we are not clear about who we are and what we are called to do.

Who contributed to the beliefs that made you who you are? Who taught you about money, success, spirituality, love, relationships, security, joy and happiness? Remember the thermometer we spoke of in chapter one? Who dictated the level of the thermometer for you? Are those beliefs in alignment with who you need to become or are they a hindrance?

We were all born into some sort of system. This system has rules, by-laws, policies, procedures, and codes of conduct created to maintain control. The greatest tool that institutions can have is to the power to maintain control of the way people think.

As children, our respective *systems* subjected us to many beliefs that have been the "stump to the elephant." An elephant is strong enough to move from a stomp from the ground, but refuses to do so due to a state of conditioning. One tool required to maintain control is ability to navigate and change perceptions. Perception is shaped by politicians, teachers, and even religious leaders. One of the most destructive uses of power I've witnessed was of individuals who took the bible out of context.

I realized most of the adults I knew had a negative outlook towards those who acquired wealth. Truth is, in most cases we felt undeserving of wealth. We were bound by a scarcity mindset and believed poverty was the only way to make it to heaven. The scripture, "Money is the root of all evil was misinterpreted as we couldn't be rich or appear to be rich. In fact, the real issue being addressed was "greed." This common misconception led bible scholars and teachers to instruct others to perceive material wealth as evil. This misconception has prevented many people from the pursuit of wealth, as if God desires that we end up a reflection of poverty and scarcity.

Another scripture often used out of context is, "the devil comes to steal, kill, and destroy." Now while there may be some setbacks in life, the manner in which you succeed is mainly dependent upon your efforts. Of course, there will be situations that are totally out of our control, however, we get to set the tone for our successes and failures. In many cases, we tend to neglect how our own beliefs and behaviors impact and influence our lives. It's not to say we don't face adversity, but if we proclaim we are made in the image of our God, who is all powerful, then the only limitations we have are the barriers within our own mind. The real enemy is a poor and ineffective belief system.

I have witnessed individuals pray about behaviors they have no intentions of changing. I'm even guilty of it myself. I prayed for a good wife while being unfaithful. I prayed to be healthier while make poor health decisions. I prayed for more money while spending all of my compensation on liabilities instead of assets. Sadly, many of us operate with this same state of conditioning and we fail to get to the root of our issues.

The brain is malleable, easily influenced, and flexible. Under certain conditions we tend to be very fickle in regards to mental energy. As a result, stigmas such as superstitions, voodoo and witch doctors have rendered individuals weak. As victims many are even willing to accept death as a verdict, because of what they were told or led to believe. On the other hand, beliefs have the capacity to be miraculous. Early Pentecostal Christians believed they could survive the bite of a venomous snake. By thought alone a person could intentionally force their bodies to reject snake poison. There is a profound truth in the concept of mind over matter. There is an even more untapped power within the mind-body connection. Even psychological therapy such as hypnosis reveal that the control center of the mind renders us unresponsive to our own actions if we don't manage our beliefs in an effective manner.

One issue that challenges our growth is that even if we have the capacity and potential to surpass great achievers and creators, something in us says, *man forget all that positive mumbo jumbo crap, let's just binge watch some Netflix and eat some pecan pie cheesecake*. That pessimistic voice questions why we are even wanting to be successful and spend time building dreams that in fact may never come to pass. This is mediocrity at its finest! What is this force?

The unconscious and subconscious mind is at war with your success. There is a contradiction between our belief system and our mindsets. There is also a distinct contradiction between what we desire and the beliefs stored within our hard drive, the subconscious mind. We will refer to it as the "control center" of the mind. The control center is where our personal narratives are written and stored as a blue print embedded in the unconscious mind. As a basis of understanding how mindsets and beliefs are formulated we will breakdown the mechanics of how all of these things work together.

Your mindset is your expectations, desires, dreams, wishes, hopes and the things you inherently believe you can achieve. Your belief system is the action, thought processes, and the intuitive instincts that guide you to achieve. For example, I can have an expectation or dream to buy my mother a home one day, but if I have a scarcity belief system my mind will never fathom me creating the type of wealth necessary to be able to do so. Vision stretches the capacity of limited thinking. The potential of your achievements is dependent upon your belief system.

Picture a vehicle that drives on four wheels. Each wheel reflects what gives us drive.

- Wheel #1 represents emotional health,
- Wheel #2 represents spiritual health,
- Wheel #3 represents social health,
- Wheel #4 represents mental health.

All four of the wheels are important to the mobility of the vehicle, but they aren't directly responsible for driving the vehicle. The engine is what gives the car mobility, however a driver must steer the vehicle and give it direction. The unconscious mind is like the engine. This is where the foundation is. The subconscious mind is the driver. It wants to use what's in the unconscious mind to get around. The way we think controls our mental, emotional, spiritual, social and even our physical health, this is why transformation starts in the mind.

Research shows that the unconscious mind[9] is developed from age's three to seven (some studies show as high as age twelve). During this stage, our minds are most susceptible to influence. It is during this period that our "value" systems are developed. Think of the young child that has to rely on another authoritarian for protection and food.

An infant is solely relying upon someone else for their survival and immediate needs which must be met by another authoritarian. Infants crave love and attention which is important in developing a sense of belonging. It is in our youth that the perception of love, security, expectations, desires, hopes and dreams are cultivated.

Depending on the environments we are raised in, our ways of thinking could be accustomed to scarcity or a

---

[9] There are many references and theories that discuss how thoughts influence behaviors and even conscious decisions. I'll leave more theories to elaborate on mind-body connections.

sense of entitlement. How we interpret the nurture or comfort of love builds upon our understanding of social environments. Our deepest aspirations become tied to what is embedded in the unconscious mind. Thoughts that are cultivated from the behavioral patterns we emulate become our "defined truth."

If you didn't acquire healthy attention, your mind may interpret it as "rejection." If you come from environment that indulged in very unhealthy eating habits while celebrating, you may continue to incorporate those habits into your adulthood. The ideal of celebration "triggers" the rewards center of the brain producing a "happy feeling." This sensation also gets woven into the unconscious mind. How we process pain, trauma, and abuse is all stored in the mind like files of neurological events. All of these behaviors, habits, feelings, and sensations get placed in our minds as a blueprint defining who we are. Our memories guide our intentions, motives, and how we process information into our thoughts.

The subconscious mind simply directs actions based on what is in the unconscious mind. Our actions, behaviors, attitudes, emotions, all transpire from the foundation built in the unconscious mind. The control center says, "Let's work hard" or "Let's just chill" based on what's grounded in our belief system.

The unconscious mind may reveal that "we value control," so the subconscious mind will exert behaviors that lead to acquiring "control." Narcissism is a behavior exerted from a desire to control. The control center[10] may communicate emotions of insecurities, motivating you to work harder so you measure up. This may lead to you feeling inadequate or defensive. These beliefs also represent the actions that should be taken in order to acquire what we define as our "standards" in life.

---

[10] Sigmund Freud: (1856–1939) An Austrian neurologist who became known as the founding father of psychoanalysis. He divided levels of human consciousness into three levels of awareness.

Challenging and questioning emotional triggers create a greater sense of introspection and self-evaluation. This is so very necessary to understand how your beliefs are shaped and how they got there in the first place. We discuss this in-depth in the next chapter.

We have the tendency to avoid emotional confrontation. I had to forgive someone and it was very difficult but the challenge was well worth the effort. We won't grow without challenging ourselves. Challenge one belief you have by subjecting it to counterintuitive behavior. Think about this in terms of your financial, emotional, belief, fear, physical health, and nutrition. What sort of belief systems have we allowed to control those areas? We must challenge those areas, here's how we might start to look at them differently.

Physical Health: Take a cold shower in the morning to shock your neurosensory glands. This requires extreme discipline, because our minds will immediately attempt to reject the command due to our state of comfort. Challenge limiting thoughts and behaviors to test your state of perceived comfort.

Financial Belief System: Test drive a car that is out of your price range. Attend a seminar that you think is out of your league. Focus on stretching your level of financial consciousness. Break one pattern of scarcity such as buying one share of stock, invest in a nonprofit of your choice, etc.

Fear Belief System: Write down one thing that frightens you. Now, test your belief system around a specific fear. I'm afraid of heights so every vacation I go zip lining. This year I even sky dived to break the conditioned perception of that fear.

For example: Write a speech and deliver it. Go live on Facebook or Instagram and talk about dream you had or some profound thought you've always wanted to share with the world. Do something you wouldn't do because of your fear of it, ride a rollercoaster.

Emotional belief system: Do something that challenges your emotions in a positive way, something that you have been negligent to try. Go on a peaceful meditation retreat, or face an emotional challenge you have been putting off.

Nutritional belief system: Try a new diet. Go vegan for 30 days, try the Keto Diet. Journal the process along with the beliefs you currently hold about eating and food.

Key Principles

> Overcoming mediocrity starts with facing our biggest competition, "our self."
> The potential of your achievements is dependent upon your belief systems.
> Our deepest aspirations become tied to what embedded in the unconscious mind.
> The subconscious mind directs our motives.
> We are entirely shaped by the things we believe.

Tools for building conscious awareness and changing your mindset may include the following:

1. **Reciting affirmations** - Introspection starts with building conscience awareness. What type of conscience thoughts do you need to create a sense of awareness around? What beliefs are preventing you from moving forward? How can you discipline your current state so you are aware of pitfalls? When we consciously and audibly describe our desires, the main objective is to align our thoughts, actions, behaviors, and vibrations with a necessary set of standards. When you quote things that are contradictory to your beliefs, you will feel challenged. The

goal is to create awareness around the beliefs that cause resistance.

Reciting and hardwiring the unconscious mind is how people are able to adopt new behaviors and change. This creates new neurological pathways in the mind so we can harness all of our energy towards a predictive outcome. This is why prayer and daily meditation over the word of God is important. We have to train our conditioned beliefs and thoughts.

It's not easy to believe you are deserving of love with pain in your heart, or that you have more than enough money with a scarcity mind set. Next, you must prepare your environment for these actions related to your beliefs. If there is a contradicting belief, the goal is to not label it negative, but to create awareness around it so you can understand it.

If you were raised seeing your mom cut out coupons and shop at thrift stores you may feel guilty trying to buy something nice for yourself. If love and affection was never shown in your home it may not be of great value unless you met someone who interpreted love through affection. These beliefs may prevent you from spoiling and celebrating the growth of your own achievements or they may keep you from connecting with others. In many cases I had to question what beliefs were damaging to my growth and potential in order to give, grow, and love on greater levels.

2. **Develop a growth mindset** - I remember my mentor invited me to a seminar that was $500. My initial thought was, "Why does it cost so much?" "I can't afford to make it to the seminar." Her response was, "You can't afford to *not* to make it to the seminar." I sat there madly upset over her lack of empathy, but the truth is I was selling myself far too short. The information I acquired at that seminar could have paid me tenfold compared to what I spent. What she

was doing was challenging me to think on a greater magnitude.

Do you have a fixed mindset or a growth mindset? Are your current aspirations causing you to become stagnant or do they challenge you to become better? When is the last time you failed at something? Do you find yourself avoiding failure? Stop it! Failure is a clear indication that you are pursuing something stretching you towards growth. We tend to have such a negative perception around failure but failure equals growth.

There are two types of mindsets: **fixed and growth**. A fixed mindset occurs when a person feels as if their set of skills, thoughts, behaviors and efforts cannot be changed or developed. This is an example of the mice that became paralyzed. Individuals with a growth mindset believe that the more time, effort and energy invested in a particular state of achievement will result in success. Therefore, while one group of individuals feel growth is impossible the other group has an underlying belief that their intelligence can grow.

A fixed mindset creates a barricade within the mind that limits a person's potential. People either feel like development is a waste of time or intelligence can't be modified. They often believe their faulty thinking is not subject to positive alteration.

Here are some tips to transition from a fixed mindset to a growth mindset:

➢ Recognize behaviors that limit your growth, and challenge weaknesses. Growth will result in resistance from either the people around you or those who have the ability to make things happen for you. Being uncomfortable is a healthy emotion necessary for challenging growth and building self-awareness.

➤ Recognize opposition as a growth opportunity. When new opportunities arise you are not supposed to avoid them. Step into the uncomfortable feeling and welcome the opportunity to learn more about yourself.

➤ Understanding the way you learn and think is very important. Everyone has different learning styles that contribute to their judgmental and rationale. Knowing how to leverage this self-discovery equips you to better understand how and why your mind is avoiding growth.

➤ Take on new challenges and expand the way you think and activate growth. Belief systems are malleable or able to be changed. Your brain has billions of cells and neuropathways that can shift, change, and grow the more you adopt new environments. Recognize the brain is not fixed, and it even processes information while we sleep.

➤ Make growth a non-negotiable in every area of your life. Be willing to conform to patterns of growth. For some this is challenging, because in many cases people are afraid to outgrow their environments.

➤ Be willing to adjust and embrace failure as a learning experience. Enjoy the journey, in life you will have plenty of "journeys." Each one is different, but the maturity that takes place within your journey is what allows your mind to expand. This is necessary for development. Each journey has a process, a procedure, and steps that are necessary as lessons in life. Simply, acknowledge that failure is a sign, and you are stepping into a new version of yourself.

- Always be led by God's vision for your life. Remember everything has a purpose and this includes what God wants to do through you and your life.

- Commit to learning, building self-awareness, and uncovering negative behaviors and patterns within yourself. This will reveal when you are stagnant and avoiding growth. Commit to attending seminars, reading books, education, and atmospheres that contribute to your growth.

- Join a mastermind group that challenges and aspires you to grow. Connect with and embrace others who also enjoy learning. This may sound cliché, but knowledge isn't power, applied knowledge is power. The individuals who are impactful and provide value are able to do so, because they use what they learn.

- Be patient with yourself and understand learning is a lifetime achievement that takes place every day of your life. Don't be hard on yourself, just work to develop grit. Some things are more difficult to grasp, while other things can be quickly learned and implemented to make change.

- Recognize that through concentrated effort, practice and learning, the art of whatever you pursue you can be successful. If someone else has done it, believe that you can do it too. Everyone has some things they are better at than others. The brain is capable of achieving so much more than most of us will settle for. Don't settle!

- Document your thoughts, processes, and plans in a journal. Watch "Who stole my cheese" to grasp the importance of tracking and writing down false beliefs that create stagnation. Journaling impresses specific important information in your subconscious mind. Taking this approach shifts your belief systems.

➤ Commit to developing new habits that will transform the person you are today into the person you were meant to be. Join a new challenge at least once a week to counter negative behavior. I practiced being vegetarian for one month and then I practiced being vegan. Soon after, I participated in a boot camp, and now I'm working toward a triathlon. Each habit you develop unravels new layers of progress that is readily available.

3. **Change your perceptions one thought at a time**. Our days are set based on the thoughts we have when we wake up or the thoughts we allow to take over our day. Have you noticed that in most cases you find what you truly desire? If you wake up and say "Today is going to be stressful," more than likely it will be stressful. If you go out in the world believing "God desires that I am successful" then you're creating a trajectory of "success." Be very careful about where your mental energy is going.

There is a concept in Quantum physics called the "observer effect[11]." The observer effect simply states that we tend to find what we are looking for. Our perceptions are created by what we give most energy towards. If you are seeking everything wrong in the world, you will find everything wrong in the world. If you are looking for opportunity, you'll find opportunity. We attract what we

---

[11] The Observer effect: In physics, **the observer effect** is the theory that simply observing a situation or phenomenon necessarily changes that phenomenon. This is often the result of instruments that, by necessity, alter the state of what they measure in some manner.

think, because our minds create a perception of consciousness based on the thoughts we have. The Wright brothers created the first flying device because their intentions and thoughts were subjected to their ability to create, not their ability to fail. What are you devoting your mental energy towards?

Of the 50,000 thoughts we have per day, most of them are all recycled thoughts. This is why most of us spend so much time stressed out because our thoughts keep us within a certain pattern of *feelings* and emotions. If you immediately wake up and think of all of the things you have to do today, rather than the goals you have to achieve, then you are placing yourself in a defensive state of belief. Anxiety, worry, and fear are stress induced beliefs associated with defensive mechanisms that back us up in a corner seeking retreat. Things we enjoy such as pleasure, joy, and happiness create thoughts that provoke our enjoyment. One state repels and the other state propels.

Take a journal and clear your mind of all of the things that are taking place in your mental space. Write down every major achievement you want to perform in the coming days. Write each action you plan to fulfill. Journal the troubling emotions, beliefs, or whatever is on your heart. You are now building awareness around your motives.

First exercise: Wake up and recite ten things you are grateful for before you begin your day. Challenge negative thoughts by writing them down in a journal and beginning to question the root cause of your perceptions. Create a thought log as a way to bring awareness to the way you feel about yourself. Deposit <u>positive thoughts in their place</u>.

Key principles and points

> - If you're not operating in an optimal state of mind your body will not produce optimal results.
> - Introspection starts with building conscience awareness.
> - There are two types of mindset, fixed and growth.
> - Commit to learning and building self-awareness to uncover negative and self-defeating behaviors and patterns within yourself.

Reshape your thought processes

In neuroplasticity[12] research (study of the brain) it was found that when we have a thought it triggers many nerves that correspond with multiple functions and impulses in the brain. When that occurs, there is an electrical exchange that occurs between neurons. When we create new thoughts, it expands the grey matter in the brain. Our brains are like plastic and able to change a desired result based on how we harness our energy. Different thoughts trigger different emotional states that have different reactions in our bodies. Our thoughts can literally heal us or they can destroy us.

As humans, we naturally project certain events in our minds based on past experiences. Often these type of decisions occur "unconsciously." This is why certain people break into hives with the thought of public speaking. There is something within their belief system that associate this event or action with a triggered emotion of nervousness and even something negative. **In most cases, the thought of facing certain situations are far more harmful than**

---

[12] I placed a Ted talk on neuroplasticity by Michael Merzenich. There is research that shows that the way we think rewires the circuitry of the brain. By thought the brain can enhance cognitive functioning and skills.

the act of facing situations, but we still become paralyzed by negative factors that may never occur.

For instance, we know facing failure is essential to success but the thought of failure keeps people from attempting anything that may result in rejection. Rejection doesn't mean everyone in the world is going to hate you but the mere thought of not being accepted is the premier core belief that surrounds the condition of this perception. The idea of rejection is more harmful than facing rejection. The thought of stress is more harmful than being in a stress-induced situation depending on how your mind interprets the idea involving stress. Knowing how to talk yourself into something that can change your life for the better is integral. A thought log may be all you need in order to go to the next level.

Now, I will walk you through how to create a thought log:

- Walk yourself through a scenario and think about its *worst case*. Now, let's begin to analyze how you can shape the outcome of that situation in your mind.
- Post positive visuals (sticky notes, photos, positive reminders) in areas you spend the most time in. Post them around your home, on your mirror, and at your work place.
- Create a sense of awareness around the thoughts you have about yourself. Repeat affirmations out loud that speak to how great you are.
- Remember God ordained you for his mission. You are a child of royalty. You are equipped, intelligent, beautiful, strong and courageous.

Considering we are capable of experiencing so many thoughts throughout the day, it's no wonder why many of us become stressed out, overwhelmed and hopelessly bombarded by negative thoughts that drain us. I went through the same thing, and upon discussing this manner with my doctor, he told me about *mindfulness.*

Practicing mindfulness is a spiritual practice of therapy that allows individuals to consciously increase awareness, aligning who we are in the present moment.

Mindfulness creates awareness through meditation, and is defined as the quality or state of being conscious or aware of something. It is a mental state achieved by focusing ones' awareness on the present moment, while calmly acknowledging and accepting ones' feelings, thoughts, and bodily sensations. You will begin to uncover a lot of thoughts that may be a hindrance to your success.

Other practices that you can use include prayer, listening to positive music, and inspirational podcasts, meditating over your vision board, doing constructive thought-provoking patterns or puzzles. These are all mind exercises.

This next section is going to sound like a neuroscience class, but I want to create a sense of awareness to show how our thoughts are tied to our emotions. Consciousness creates empowerment. It's not just ignorance that keeps us disadvantaged, but unawareness of how to leverage our own psyche is also a hindrance to growth. With this information, you can own your own thoughts, dictate your own mindset, and your emotions through awareness. You have the power to own the atmosphere in which you are *called to create.*

Think Positive. Speak Life. Breed love. Embody Compassion. Enrich others.

As you go through your day ask yourself these questions:
1. Are the thoughts I'm having bringing me closer to my dreams?
2. Are these thoughts beneficial to my growth?
3. Are these thoughts producing the results I need to further my endeavors?

4. Are these thoughts bringing me peace?
5. If I am having negative thoughts, how can I abandon them to take ownership of my day?

Negative thoughts left unattended and unresolved will cause catastrophic damage limiting our time on earth and the work we are called here to do. It is time to take control of the biggest weapon you have--- your mind.

Use Words of power to replace negative thoughts

I enjoy using power words because when you apply power words it builds certainty. No one can build a foundation on unsteady ground. Would you build your home on something substantial or something flimsy with very little support? Absolutely not. This is why I like what Mohammed Ali said about being the greatest. He spoke it and affirmed it until it became true in his mind. His words confirmed what he believed to be true, and that's what *power words* do.

Words such as can't, maybe, someday, probably, hate, and every other negative word creates resistance. You know what happens when I use these words? My mind is finding a way to rationalize being a loser. For example, you call a friend to ask them to hang out, and their response is "I don't know, I will let you know later." Does that sound certain at all? To me, it sounds like a complete cop-out. In fact, if I know the person well, I already know what will happen later. I know it's a cop-out, because it's my **golden go-to** when I don't want someone to feel rejected. It's also a way for me to maintain the *people pleaser mindset*. The reality is, these kinds of responses are undependable, and this is the kind of talk you are shaping your beliefs with when you operate this way.

Words can contribute to us being insecure. Insecurity occurs when standards don't match expectations.

Consistency towards breaking down barriers has to become a key factor in your progression. When your inner dialogue don't match what you want to experience, there's a disconnect between your body and soul. You'll make excuses not to commit which results in a loss of self-confidence. When you affirm yourself, it builds mental strength, you'll program your mind for success by impressing powerful affirmations into your subconscious mind.

What are some powerful words and phrases?

Words like I can, I will achieve, I am destined to fulfill, I am a winner, instead of negative self-talk. Anything positive that helps you to maintain your authority in the battlefield. Instead of copping out, tell your friend you have plans, and if your plans change you will let them know. Stop letting yourself down with weak words. Abolish mindsets that are destructive to your growth. Make a list of the damaging thought patterns that hinder your growth and how you feed into them. I've listed examples of mindsets and behaviors that follow them:

Mindset type	Results
The "scarcity" mindset	Limited thinking in an abundant world
The "microwave" mindset	Wanting things right now
The "overdramatizing" mindset	Expecting things to be worse than they really are
The "doubtful" mindset	Lacking expectation of positive outcomes
The "generalization" mindset	Perception that everyone is the same

The "luck" mindset	Everything that happens to people comes from luck
The "toxic" mindset	Having dirty, filthy, unhealthy thoughts
The "sinful" mindset	Any vain imagination against the will of God
The "oppressed" mindset	Feeling or behaving with a bondage mentality
The "big picture" mindset	Focusing on the big picture so much you don't value the details
The "victim" mindset	Everything that happens is always someone else's fault
The "Joneses" mindset	The belief that you have to keep up with trends
The "egocentric" mindset	Bigotry, egotistic, narcissist
The "My way or the highway" mindset	Accepting no other ideas or suggestions but my own
The "Crab in a bucket" mindset	The desire to bring others down because you don't want to see others succeed.

Now, think about and journal about the destructive mindsets holding you back?

Key principles and points

> Creating new thoughts expand the grey matter of the mind changing the biology of the brain-plasticity.
> Mindfulness is a practice in which we consciously increase awareness
> The law of reciprocity ensures that when we open ourselves up to help someone else, our hands are open to receive, this is called reciprocation.

Now that we have journeyed through mindsets and beliefs systems the next important barrier to uncover is emotional health.

Action tools in order:

1. Recite affirmations.
2. Develop a growth mindset.
3. Create a thought journal.
4. Use words of power to replace negative thoughts.
5. Abolish mindsets that are destructive to your growth.

CHAPTER FOUR-THE BARRIERS OF BROKEN EMOTIONS

Your worst enemy can be your
best advocate. You can allow
fear to rule over you or use it to
fuel your passion.

Fourth Barrier to mediocrity: lack of knowledge of emotional intelligence

The Fourth Barrier to mediocrity is the lack of knowledge and emotional intelligence. Your worst enemy can be your best advocate. *You can allow fear to rule over you or use it to fuel your passion.* Emotional intelligence[13] (EI) is the awareness of ones' own emotions as well as the emotional conditions of others around us. EI proposes high significant value because the more we understand ourselves and others around us the better we can serve each other. Not recognizing dysfunctional emotional patterns could be the most significant barrier standing in the way of achieving your goals. Understanding how your emotions and feelings shape perspectives is vital to being present and aware.

Negative emotions can have a detrimental impact on identity, vision and mindset:

---

[13] Emotional Intelligence is the ability to understand emotions in ourselves and others. I placed a Ted talk on this topic as well to elaborate at end of book in footnotes.

- Identity: Negative emotions contribute to imposter syndrome[14], a psychological sense of inadequacy that tells a person they don't belong to a certain group. This can cause you to dismiss your own achievements and accomplishments, while preventing you from joining individuals you deserve to be in the room with.
- Vision: Negative emotions can influence you to believe you aren't worthy of the goals you have established for yourself. If you are not careful, this can cause you to stay in the past rather than design the future you know you want for yourself.
- Mindset: Negative emotions can place a deep emphasis on bias or rumination. This causes individuals to focus solely on all the negative attributes of yourself and others.

Positive, negative or neutral feelings and emotions impact everything we do or don't do in some sort of way, so it's only right we discuss how this worked in my journey. **Fear is one of the main barriers that prevents people from pursuing their dreams**. Fear paralyzes individuals by influencing them to stay in their comfort zone. This type of fear isn't a fear of imminent threat, but rather a false imaginary that something negative *could* occur.

There are many different types of fear, but the two most common types are associated with moving forth. They are fear of failure and fear of rejection. Fear of failure keeps us from trying new things and fear of rejection creates a false sense of abandonment, we believe that people won't accept us and we simply won't measure up.

---

[14] Imposter syndrome: "A psychological phenomenon in which people are unable to internalize their accomplishments."

We are naturally wired to desire a connectedness, so the idea that we won't be accepted is deadly to the psyche.

You see, before the thought or manifestation of trying a new venture, journey, business, idea, or a worthy ambition, fear is already at the door waiting for you. Fear is going to try to overturn your reasoning of any logical explanation to pursue something better. Even in relationships, we are often misguided. How many times have you known someone to fall into lust believing they are in love, just for the relationship to end in regret? God compels us to be pure and patient. Our hormones sound back, "But I think I'm in love." Time often reveals the impulsive decision and it often ends in regret.

When we are chasing our dreams, our minds tell us we're getting no results, and that we should just quit. But, the heart says to keep pressing on. Feelings can cause each of us to make irrational decisions, view a situation out of context, or to make impulsive decisions that lead to our downfall.

We live in a society where dysfunctional emotional abuse is normalized. Gang violence, poverty, and substance abuse was normal in my environment. Abuse stems from anger, fear of growth leads to poverty, lust leads to destruction, pride causes division, unmanaged anxiety leads to overwhelming stress, and boredom results in a lack of passion.

Emotional intelligence is a skill and a gift that can allow you to maneuver certain emotional states to improve both interpersonal and intrapersonal relationships. Being able to effectively analyze, understand, and fully comprehend different emotional states from interpersonal and intrapersonal relations, is proven to be a vital skill in social relations. Feelings are nothing more than communication expressed within the body that is conveyed from an expression of our beliefs. Our biggest downfall is lack of awareness in how emotions influence our actions.

How emotions impact behaviors

It's important to note that no one is exempt from the influence of emotions. Emotions have blinded the logic of some of the most intelligent individuals in the country and has since the beginning of time. Examples include some of the most detrimental events in America such as the financial crisis in 2008. Some of the smartest individuals encouraged millions to invest in *dummy* bonds. People unknowingly invested their life savings on the merit of untrustworthy individuals. People suspended all logic for the chance to receive economic gains.

The power of lust has influenced individuals to go against their better judgement, even sacrificing their legacies for temporary fulfillment. Pride has caused some of the world's most powerful leaders to sacrifice their followers to appease their own egos. If you think this is just an issue of modern times, you couldn't be more wrong. King David sent his own soldier into combat to die, so he could commit adultery with his wife.

I don't want to paint emotions as the enemy, because they serve an important aspect of our survival. Emotions indicate when there are imposing threats that can place us in harm. Emotions tell us when to eat and when we are full. Even that gut feeling comes in handy when something feels out of place, like telemarketers trying to scam you into sending your credit card information in exchange for millions of dollars. Let's face it, sometimes we need emotions to make the best decisions possible for our lives, while others times they lead us to ruin.

The best thing you can do for yourself is to become conscious of negative emotions. Recognizing when you are in danger, or threatened is important. Fear of failure, rejection, poverty, and acceptance paralyzes us and can prevent us from moving forward. Feelings are nothing more than a form of communication, an inner illustration of our thoughts. There is power in how we utilize our emotional states to create a desired outcome. It depends on how we leverage this form of energy. Fear is most often presented in a negative manner, but fear can build caution and wisdom. Before we address how fear can be a positive force, let's first evaluate "negative bias."

Our minds naturally tend to focus on the negative. Negative news spreads faster than positive stories. As we go through our day we often tend to reflect on anything negative before we replay positive encounters even if they brought us joy. Why is that? Our brains are wired to help us survive, it's a defensive mechanism. The nervous system has done an incredible job evolving over millions of years since the day we lived as Homo sapiens.

Early civilization required us to go out and hunt for food. Our whole sense of survival was dependent upon our effectiveness to acquire food and maintain safety. Safety includes security and protection from harm. Harm includes any external threats from animals, other human beings, and the environment. Any mistake could result in death. As civilization evolved the natural tendency to evaluate any negative factors is still a default setting in our minds.

Our minds project fear to escape vulnerability. It's the reason why we face physiological resistance such as procrastination, avoiding confrontation, or the natural tendency to stay confined to a comfort zone. Anger arises when we feel threatened, attacked or when we experience indifference such as social inequality or disrespect. Just like anger and fear, love and joy are also an expression. Love and joy align with passion and fulfillment. I learned recently that positivity activates stem cells in the body which strengthens the immune system. Smile more, you live longer, and more importantly--- God desires us to experience joy. It's a scientific proven fact!

Fear as a Motivator

Fear can cause you to plan out every detail in your life to limit failure rather than abandon a goal. Fear can cause you to protect your integrity through Gods word. As mentioned in the last section, fear can be a greatest instinctual motivator to achieve success. Fear can be a healthy emotion if it is leveraged properly.

In order to leverage our emotions to advance in the world, we must acquire a greater sense of introspection. This means conducting a strict self-analysis. You must develop emotional consciousness. Introspection means looking at patterns objectively rather than through an emotional lens. Introspection occurs when one is objective in evaluating their emotions logically.

As stated earlier, it is important to analyze your feelings through mindfulness. When you are fully aware and in tune with your body, mind and spirit, you can listen to your body. Improving emotional intelligence improves self-management and also provides clarity for social awareness. This requires some listening and observing of your own thoughts, and being conscious of others around you.

As an example, someone said something disrespectful to me and it made me furious. The only thing on my mind was how I was going to respond. After a moment I began to analyze the emotion I was having, and I thought, "Why am I so angry right now?" The only power that this emotion has is the authority I had given it. I felt angry based on the associations I had given to the emotion. I then began to question why I gave this person that type of power over me. No matter how this person made me feel they didn't take anything tangible from me. They were only responding from a level of consciousness based on a perception that was more than likely flawed. I thanked God for the awareness and the ability to operate from a higher consciousness. I was also thankful that I did not let anyone rob me of the joy God said was mine.

My childhood experiences were the reason I didn't know how to effectively manage my emotions. This type of mindset pours over into other areas of life. It is also important to note, impulsive behaviors lead to making poor choices rather than decisions based on logic, sound doctrine, wisdom, or instinct.

Just as mental and financial health wasn't discussed, emotions were never really a topic of discussion in our home growing up. We come from a generation of males who regarded it as weak to show emotions, they saw vulnerability as toxic. Due to this flawed belief, we spent more time abandoning feelings and suppressing healthy emotions. Sometimes it was covered by substance abuse or other addictive behaviors.

When escapism is the resolution to these conditions they are rarely resolved. Unresolved issues and behaviors are buried, and research shows that in the long run these things cause far more harm than good. The meaning behind certain mental conditions determine how we manage ourselves during these circumstances.

Narcissism[15] is a behavior that can be both healthy and toxic. Contrary to popular belief, it can serve as a basis of something healthy, based on intention and motives. This requires you as an individual to be clear on what you value. Great leaders are ultimately willing to adjust their behavior, in an effort to create a positive outcome. Toxic narcissism on the other hand, is destructive and will provoke one to degrade others to edify themselves. When this occurs individuals make themselves victims by intentionally shaping perspectives for their own personal gain.

Healthy Narcissism

As a husband, father, and leader I value nothing more than building great relationships with my wife,

---

[15] Healthy narcissism is the ability to have self-worth and value for yourself to give it to others. Having compassion for yourself allows you to clearly care for yourself to give even more comfort to help others become successful Toxic Narcissism causes a lack of empathy for others while have dysfunctional behaviors and poor emotions patterns that results in negative outcomes.

children, and team. This is a priority in my life. In order for this to occur, I have to effectively manage my emotions. As easy as this sounds it was terribly difficult for me. For one, I didn't recognize how the abuse I endured had impacted me. Secondly, my wife could make one gesture or ask a question such as, "Babe did you take out the trash?" and I'd be triggered. If I made a mistake, I would automatically shut down as if I was being degraded. Every mistake I made was internalized as "I am a failure," so I told her she was "nagging." You could say--- I felt "emasculated" as if she had stripped me of my masculinity. I'm sure you can probably tell, there were many emotional hurdles I had to overcome. That doesn't even include my angry outbursts. I lacked balance, I was either hypersensitive or overly aggressive. Imagine me taking over the role as a leader of a team. Emotional intelligence has been a critical component to my growth and healing.

My wife and I have a blended family, and one of the most difficult challenges I had to overcome was building a relationship with *our* daughter. I came into her life when she was about the age of four. Prior to that, the only man that had been in her life was her father. I noticed when she came around me she was very uncomfortable. She shut down and become defensive. When her father and I were in the same room she felt a sense of "guilt" for being kind to me. On the other hand, sometimes I felt a sense of resentfulness if her father let her down in any way. Overall, I felt stuck between a rock and a hard place. Even asking her to clean her room was like climbing a mountain because of the tension between us.

Because I had a healthy state of narcissism, I challenged myself to acquire approval from her. The root cause of the problem was her struggle to find and attain a sense of identity between her father and me. She felt like I was intruding upon her territory, or placing division in what she'd always known, so she shut down emotionally. She didn't have the level of intellectual maturity required to effectively convey how she was feeling. I had to come with an approach that was different from what I was taught growing up. It took me back to the *growth mindset*, and I knew I had to be flexible.

This required me to humble myself while taking time to emotionally engage myself in her world. When she became defensive I went into protective mode. I evaluated her body language. I asked permission to come into her world to build relationship. Sometimes I even had to play princess and tea cup to be a part of her imaginary world. By doing this I aligned myself with the emotional state of consciousness she was feeling. Of course, we can't have a dirty kingdom. Come on, a dirty kingdom? What princess has a dirty kingdom? She smiled, agreed and we cleaned up together. Over time our bond was developed and strengthened. She began to tell me her fears. I would go into "coach mode." I empowered her. If she felt grief and worry, I went into "refuge mode." I provided her with affirmations and painted a picture of reality that helped her understand that God is a provider and that she is a warrior.

Healthy narcissism is great for leadership. It causes us as leaders to understand how to effectively manage those we are serving. In this case it was my daughter, but this also applies to managing a team. In the past, I shut down and felt rejected and became defensive. I eventually realized nothing was being solved. By first taking inventory of how we were both feeling, including nonverbal cues such as body language, I become attentive to her values and she mine.

I had to think about what her needs and dreams were. What did she need? How could I effectively submerge myself in her world to get her to comply with my overall objectives? How can we create an atmosphere of mutual success? Of course, as a man I needed to know I could fix whatever was wrong, even if it meant being humble to figure it out. This healthy state of narcissism is something all great leaders have, however you must also be aware of when narcissism become toxic.

Toxic Narcissism

When I became an adult, I asked my father why he was so abusive. He said his mother disciplined him in the same manner that he disciplined me. My grandmother was a severe alcoholic. There was no such thing as an emotional bond, because to him being vulnerable was weak. Even when I cried at my brother's funeral I was influenced to be silent.

When I felt joy my father tore me down. When I felt confident, he wouldn't show up to any of my events. In his mind anyone else experiencing joy meant that he was losing something vital to whom he was. This caused him to destroy any celebratory moment for others, even if he had to make himself the victim.

When my father cheated on his wife with another woman in their home, he fabricated a whole story saying she cheated first. He created fake stories to rationalize poor behavior so people felt sorry for him. This is the opposite of healthy narcissism. Instead of aligning himself with others he manipulated people to only see his perspective. Adults who suffer from chronic narcissism often shows signs of resentfulness even late in life. I posted on Facebook about "insecurities" in other human beings and was made to feel bad by a sly comment he made. It really disturbed me. I couldn't understand it. Even the mentioning of me writing a book annoyed him. During a counseling session, his new wife asked him about the abuse I suffered, and he said he felt jealous of the success his children was acquiring. That's when it dawned on me. This individual has been living in a state of toxic narcissism and feels threatened by other peoples' success.

I have seen this behavior in others as well. My friend's mother recently came into an inheritance and bought my friend a car. My friend's husband was upset at how happy his wife had become. He degraded her and the car saying she was stupid for taking the gift and the car was ugly. He grew furious at the attention she was getting and became abusive. Eventually he physically damaged the car. Maybe it threatened his sense of masculinity because he didn't buy it, but the more she became enthusiastic, the more furious he became with jealousy and envy.

Toxic narcissism occurs when an individual makes themselves feel as if they are a victim. On the contrary, healthy narcissism occurs as a result of placing other people intentions, wellbeing and success before your own to help them achieve a goal so that everyone wins. It's important to become aware of emotional "triggers."

The Five Love Languages was written by Gary Chapman, it simply states that individuals have five key traits that conveys love. We all have a certain way that we need to receive love. Chapman lists the five key love languages: Words of affirmation, quality time, receiving gifts, acts of service, and physical touch. Based on his research, when one of these acts are performed, individuals feel valued, loved, and appreciated. My love languages are words of affirmation and physical touch. If my wife gives me a compliment I feel like I'm walking on clouds for at least a week. If she touches me, it's over… I melt. It's crazy. If she buys me gifts I appreciate it, but it's not near as impactful as a physical touch or verbal expression of appreciation. Each one of these acts' "trigger" certain emotions in me.

Still, if my wife questions me multiple times about a particular subject it triggers a sense of inadequacy in me. It feels like a lack of trust, confidence in my skills, or competence in my knowledge. More than anything, it feels like she is questioning my character, judgement, and well-being. Sometimes I lash out, because what is conveyed is, *I am not measuring up to her set of standards.* You have to become aware of what "words, or verbiage" strikes certain emotional states.

Sometimes it's even a sensory thing, for me, smelling certain alcohols take me take to times when domestic violence happened in my childhood. When I see a child being abused, it takes me back to my childhood. Then there are things that shift my mind towards joy. When I eat catfish, it reminds me of my grandmother's cooking. When I see the beach, it reminds me of the first time I took my family on a vacation.

You too, can develop an inventory and learn to recognize what triggers certain emotions. What brings you joy, passion, anger, grief, peace, and fulfillment?

Take inventory of your life, outlook, and current journey to lead you to self-discovery. Asking questions such as:

- Times when I am at peace
- Environment that cause me the most stress involve:
- The moments I have the most joyful times are:
- I am most fulfilled when I am
- I feel good about myself when

These questions will help you get clear about what generates impact in your life and what triggers your emotions. It will be important to practice being aware of both. A good indicator of a *trigger* alarm is when you recognize your heart rate is elevated. When you are in fight or flight mode 70% of the blood rushes from the amygdala and flows through other areas of your body. The blood flows to your legs and arms until you reach a place safety.

Willpower is most sustainable when we our heart rate is low, thus reinforcing the power and benefits of meditation. When a person takes a deep breath and slows down, the mind, heart rate, and willpower increases significantly. This switches the emotional state of the mind. You must first test the thoughts associated with events and environments. Here's a model I received from a great therapist I had the pleasure of spending time with. It exhibits how events trigger thoughts, emotions, and outcomes.

When a negative event takes place, you first begin to think about the event, then there will be an emotional experience. If you replace the negative thought with a positive thought, the outcome will be different. Think about this, when an argument takes place, there are usually thoughts associated. Based on the situation, the can lead to different outcomes.

Example: <u>Someone steps on your foot by accident:</u>

➢ Thoughts about the situation including past trauma may "trigger" fight or flight.
➢ If you have negative thoughts about the person or situation, you may likely recall past situations.
➢ Negative emotions flow, leading to a negative outcome.

Let's say you replace the thought with something positive, such as "I am sure they meant no harm." Fight or flight now becomes pause and plan, your heart rate slows down, and you have greater clarity about the situation, and are able to orchestrate a positive outcome.

You can literally talk yourself into a better mindset. Let's talk about anxiety, it occurs when one feels a lack of control or uncertainty. When someone develops anxiety, they challenge the mental state by creating a visual psychological map. Usually, they start by walking themselves through a series of questioning to understand the outcome of a situation. Then, in most cases, the anticipation of an event causes more distress than the actual event. What we fear, we create.

Situation: Anxiety is high due to a new business opportunity, finances are scarce and you must deliver a great speech to win a major deal. What could go wrong when you enter the room? Using a *then what* line of questioning allows your mind to picture a situation step by step. This procedure reduces the heart rate and encourages will power and positive instinctual behavioral that usually result in positive outcomes. Here is an example of how you could potentially talk yourself through this situation:

You may think: Someone could recognize me from a bad experience.

Ask yourself: Then what? *I may have to explain my past and also why I am there.*

Continue with the then what line of questioning:

Then what? *That person may report a past of negative behavior that speaks to my character.*

Then what? *I will set up a second meeting to maintain my sense of professionalism.*

Then what? *They may decline hearing my response and I'll lose the deal.*

Then what? *I'll have to find another job opportunity.*

Then what? *I'll find another job and continue pursuing success.*

This tool will allow you to frame events mentally, and to acquire a sense of control. Try it, the next time you feel overwhelmed or are experiencing anxiety.

Some emotional reactions such as anger are derived from an underlying belief. An illustration that explains this concept is the iceberg theory. The iceberg theory states that everything seen on the surface has occurred as a result of something dwelling within us (unresolved issues, beliefs, expectations, or traumas).

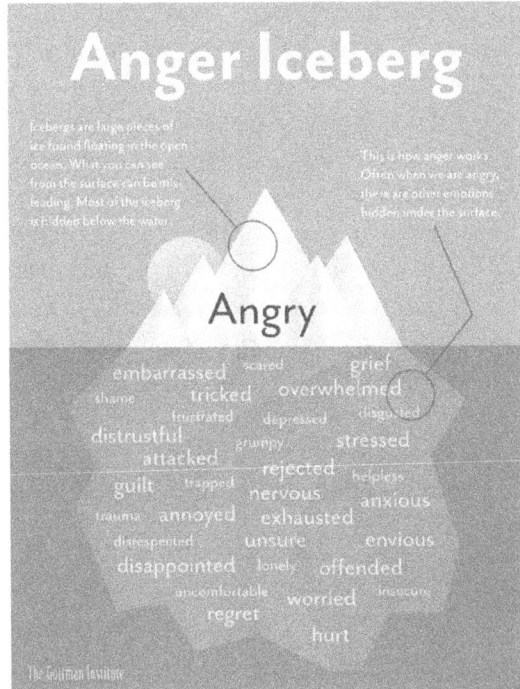

Anger Iceberg

Icebergs are large pieces of ice found floating in the open ocean. What you can see from the surface can be misleading. Most of the iceberg is hidden below the water.

This is how anger works. Often when we are angry, there are other emotions hidden under the surface.

Angry

embarrassed scared grief
shame tricked overwhelmed
frustrated depressed disgusted
distrustful grumpy stressed
attacked
guilt trapped rejected helpless
nervous
trauma annoyed exhausted anxious
disrespected unsure envious
disappointed lonely offended
uncomfortable insecure
worried
regret
hurt

The Gottman Institute

Iceberg theory concluded that 10% of socially acceptable behaviors are revealed through emotional responses, while 90% of our reactions stem from an underlying condition or underlying unresolved problem. To overcome something, you have to address the issue that hide beneath the surface.

Insecurity results from a lack of experience or confidence in oneself. Some people are insecure, because they have not had a relationship with a parent or their parent neglected them. This has created a need to have control from unmet expectations causing individuals to lash out when they are triggered by something.

For example, an argument breaks out between two people stemming from a misunderstanding where someone feels disrespected. The person that is feeling disrespected is angry about something much more profound than the act of being disrespected. The anger stems from something within their beliefs, or maybe even unmet expectations that haven't been dealt with. This event just "triggered" the response.

In my own marriage, I recognized specific triggers that led me to believe that I had lost something in certain situations that I preferred to end in another way. The feeling of insecurity occurred as a lack of control over certain situations. In many cases, I hadn't matured enough to be comfortable in my role as a man. This condition resulted from childhood traumas that hadn't been addressed. You will not have control over every situation in your life.

Locus of Control

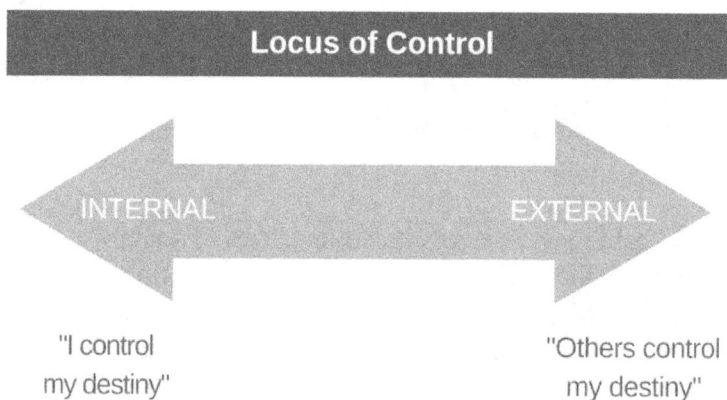

INTERNAL   EXTERNAL

"I control   "Others control
my destiny"   my destiny"

Let's talk about some concepts that may be able to help you have some sort of control. The external locus versus internal locus of control. The external locus of control means, *they control my life,* and an internal locus of control means *I control my life.*

American psychologist Julian Rotter[16] is known for this social influence theory. Those who possess high levels of internal locus of control feel empowered to create their own destiny, resulting in self-assurance. Those who have lived by an external locus of control contribute their success or fate to external forces outside of their power, this is a victim mentality. Each side of the external and internal locus of control has its own pros and cons which we will discuss below.

Breakdown of internal/external locus- Pros vs. Cons
Pros:

External: These individuals are typically stuck in victim mode and have not tapped into their own power. They may also have clarity on how external forces can impact goals. Their perception of reality is that the outside has more control and power than they possess within them leading to lower levels of motivation and drive.
Internal: These individuals are tapped into their own power, and tend to be self-efficient, goal and action-oriented.

---

[16] Julian Rotter (born 22 October 1916) is an American psychologist who is known for developing influential theories, including social learning theory and locus of control.

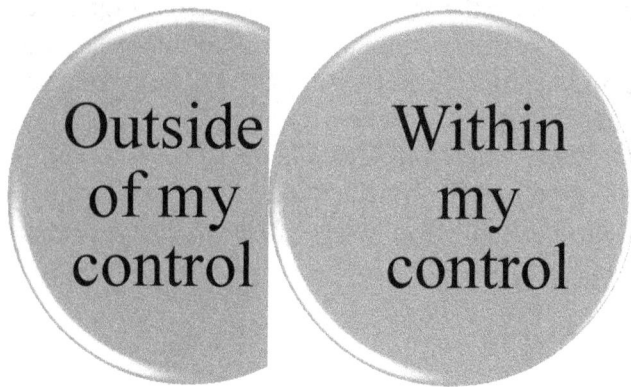

Cons: These individuals have trouble delegating and they rush ahead of Gods' will for their life. This leads to blaming themselves when unfortunate events occur outside of their control or when a failure happens.

The goal is to develop a safe balance while also recognizing some things are out of your control. We can't control the weather, but we can get a rain jacket and umbrella when the storm persists.

Do things happen to you or do you happen to things?
Some things in life we have no control over, but recognizing how we are affected by those things increase the level of success and furthers the probability of a positive outcome.

Take your power back and don't allow fear to paralyze you. Ask yourself what you could do next if something negative were to occur. You can do this by creating step by step action plans: This removes the negative feedback loop from your brain.

What methods do you follow to handle stress and what does stress mean to you?

Emotional intelligence can also be useful in recognizing what your emotions are telling you. Emotions are nonverbal and verbal expressions of self. From birth we are masters of lip service. Even children are great at lying and manipulating, but emotions are seen in body language. The most successful people excel by learning how to leverage their emotions through a state of awareness. One of the best skills you can possess will take you very far, and that is to master the art of relating to others.

By now I'm sure you have concluded that emotions are one thing we all have in common. Being actively present in the moment can be a superpower if you can manage your emotions. We connect through feelings. We are able to have compassion for each other. Emotions play a vital role in connecting and engaging. In order to master this task, you must take inventory of the different emotional states you are experiencing through psychoanalysis.

Emotional intelligence became such an essential role in my life over the past few years. Mainly for two critical reasons, my health and my role in leadership. Growing up, we never sought out any form of therapy nor did we discuss *emotions* in the home. You can imagine the overwhelming inadequacy I felt when I was told to seek out professional help for depression and anxiety.

Whether fear, anxiety, depression, or worry, we all experience feeling powerless at some point in our lives. It wasn't until I began to journal what I was feeling and to place a label on it, that I began to change my mindset. I needed to grasp a sense of awareness so I could overcome my situation. I don't know if it's common, but it challenged growth in me and I'm sure in others also. Some of us hold on to traumatic situations but, we are called to control our emotions not allow them to control us. True overcomers are masters of self. Don't let emotions drive you, take back the keys to the vehicle.

If you feel your best, you can do your best, in order for that to occur you have to pursue peak emotional health. Your health can be greatly affected by fear and the anxiety it causes. Imagine what life would look like it we no longer had to be captive to fear. I am not referring to the type of fear caused by being in imminent danger, but I am referring to fear of rejection or failing at an opportunity that could change your life.

Do you believe emotions are mechanically engineered based on the perception we give them? What if emotions only possessed authority based on the labels we placed on them? This concept and idea could create a paradigm shift. One person may view pain as a significant setback, another person interprets it as a vehicle to get from where they are to victory.

There are two great motivational conditions that provoke action, they are extreme pain or trauma. This could include things such as hitting rock bottom or experiencing pain or inspiration like death or love. When a person loses everything and hits rock bottom something in them shifts and provokes them to action. Love is a powerful emotion in which one supersedes everything in them to express and experience their highest vibration. In these moments human beings are able to achieve far more than they would under normal emotional conditions.

I thought about this when I saw a martial art expert chopping a brick in half. The average individual wouldn't dare attempt such an incredible act because of pain associated with this task. This expert was conditioned to compartmentalize pain differently, completely focused on the result. Pain still exists, but instead of confronting the pain they manage it mentally. Understanding how to manage pain is a by-product of emotional intelligence.

Take fear for instance. Have you ever been afraid to do something for the first time and then after repeating the act, the fear decreased? I experienced this recently with my daughter at White Water. When we went on a rollercoaster the first time she was petrified. She grabbed my wrist and held on tight. Every swing, turn and dip placed her in a state of fear. My daughter cried, and I held her until the end of the ride. She didn't want to get on any more rollercoasters after that. I mean can you blame her?

When we went back to whitewater a second time, she went on the rollercoaster and found some excitement, and wasn't nearly scared as the first experience. She actually found it fun. The third time was a breeze ---there was no sense of panic, anxiety or hesitation in getting on the roller-coaster, now she beats me to the line. The thrill of the excitement took time, but by the third time, I began to notice she was no longer afraid of the rollercoaster ---she was anxious to try another ride.

Imagine, a lion crouches in the woods slowly maneuvering the woodland seeking to dominate its dessert, including everything in it--- the zebra. Once the zebra recognizes an immediate threat, adrenaline fills its body as it shifts into fight or flight mode. The zebra then flees to escape the barbarian. Its heart is beating, inducing a higher state of focus and concentration contributing to the emotional state. The zebra sprints at phenomenal speeds to escape its predator. Once it regains its position among its habitat other zebras surround it reducing the stage of frantic panic. Once the zebra identifies its social support it forgets the threat, the memory of its condition, and relaxes, solely focused on the atmosphere rather than memories they play back over and over. This is the natural tendency we as humans are more prone to adopt. Just like zebras have triggers so do we as human beings, zebras focus on the atmosphere rather than the memories or experiences that tend to replay in a loop causing more stress and worry to the mind and body.

I remember taking public speaking for the first time. The emotional state of fear was literally polarizing for some of the students on day one. However as each student became skilled and familiar with the process of speaking the sense of fear began to diminish overtime. Eventually, the power of familiarity is created and we can experience *systematic desensitization.*

Familiarity empowers you to overcome barriers that once existed. It's because as you continue with the action repeatedly, it builds awareness in your mind and belief system. If you want to impress something great upon your subconscious mind, act is if you have been there already and done it before, it will place your mind in a relaxed state reduce anxiety. Psychologists use a similar technique to help patients by using *virtual reality.* I've used it often in sales and to overcome stage fright. Even though I'm a chatty patty and a social butterfly, I got nervous speaking in front of people. I had to become aware of the feeling of fear, call it out and conquer it. Eventually after speaking in front of people, this was no longer a fear of mine. After doing something for so long you will have the confidence and belief system engrained within your mind. Emotions can be manipulated in order to succeed where others have failed. Breakthrough can occur when you push past your fear.

Fear of Success and Fear of Failure
I was raised and conditioned to have a poverty-stricken mindset. We didn't have the best education in public school, nor did we have access to good mental health facilities. In most cases I had succumbed to being mediocre because I was afraid of success. Fear of failure will cause you to stay in the same position because you are afraid of not being able to handle more responsibility, fame, or being seen. If you have the same story, you will have to question the inadequacy. Saying it out loud helps to create new thought patterns in your mind.

I have seen this work first hand in my life. I still have to face self-sabotaging behaviors that limit what I am capable of achieving. There is a great tool called *Take 5* that helps overcome this barrier.

The five most common senses are sight, hearing, taste, smell, and touch. When you are facing experiences that challenge you mentally you can use this exercise to help you overcome these challenges by creating awareness.

Take Five (5)
What are **five** things I can see?
What are **four** things I can hear?
What are **three** things you would like to taste or can taste?
What are **two** things you can feel?
What is **one** thing you can smell?
This shifts brain activity from the limbic system and amygdala to prefrontal cortex where rational decision making takes place. This is another heart variation tool to improve will power.

Adopt environments that encourage you to create the best results

Research has shown that not being able to effectively manage stress has been tied to memory loss, diabetes, cancer, strokes, and other heart diseases. Overall this state of conditioning has plagued humanity for centuries. For those who have learned to channel the energy into other areas this is a well-known advantage. Visual exploration is a great tool to navigate through the battlefield of our emotions.

Dr. Robert Sapolsky[17] wrote about this in his book, "Why Zebras don't get Ulcers." This book is a great illustration of how effective social support creates a positive outlook when someone is stressed out. Environments play a critical role in shifting perspective to create more success while preserving the psychological

---

[17] Robert M. Sapolsky, Ph.D., is the John A. and Cynthia Fry Gunn Professor of Biological Sciences and a professor of neurology and neurological sciences at Stanford University. I have included a Ted Talk speech over the effects of stress and biology in the Appendix.

state of belonging. In groups and friendships, we quickly realize that we all experience the same issues. Open dialogue allows you to speak and create a predictable outcome. When you do this, you are naturally reducing your heart rate and improving awareness. Through social support you can also gain insight about other triggers that you may not be aware of.

1. Challenge the thoughts that cause you stress and trauma.
2. Write down triggers and create awareness of what causes fight or flight responses.
3. Practice mindfulness through prayer, meditation, yoga, affirmations, and other healthy practices.
4. Meditate on positive visions to expand neuropathways in your mind.
5. Leverage a positive environment to improve awareness.
6. Adopt a growth mindset and recognize you always have the ability to grow.
7. Keep a thought log to challenge thoughts of insecurity or other beliefs that are contrary to your growth.
8. Walk in and own your joy!

Fear is the only thing standing between you and your goals. For this reason, I composed a set of tools to help you discover the nature of your emotional health. First let's discuss how we attain peak emotional states.

Four Pillars of Good Emotional Health:
1. **Physical Health**
It's flex season baby. Get outside and get some sun, exercise, sweat and train your body. Exercising makes you feel happier, reduces stress, releases dopamine, and research shows that it's builds mental health as well. When you look good, you feel good. Jim Rohn further validates

this phrase with his quote, "There is nothing more pitiful than a ready and willing mind but an incapable body."

2. Mental Health
Just like good physical health, mental health is vital. Meditate, and improve mindfulness by being present. Recognize the challenging ques of stress as well as anything harmful to your head space. The benefits of good mental health include less anxiety and depression, sharper memory and clarity of focus. When these are improved you experience improved self-esteem, joy, and livelihood. The inability to control stress responses is what leads to poor health conditions such as cancer, heart disease and other health problems.

3. Nutrition and its Importance
Putting the wrong gas in your vehicle will ruin it. It is the same way with our bodies, if we put the wrong food in our bodies, we will ruin it. It is a fact that the food we eat impacts our mental and emotional health. If we want to improve the peak states of our emotional health we have to put the right ingredients in our bodies. Microbiomes are small microorganisms, they are connected to our minds and affect our stomachs. These small organisms protect us from germs, regulate our immune systems, and release and retain energy.

4. Sleep health
When you are rested you are charged up to seize the day. On most days, I tend to wake up as early as three a.m. to exercise and meditate, but I have learned the value of rest. Much of my anxiety was due to a restless mind, both of these cause fatigue. Our bodies cannot heal without rest. Sleep improves cognitive function, disposes of toxins in the body, and regulates every cell within the body. Sleep has been shown to be more impactful for weight loss than exercise and diet.

Each emotion we experience poses an opportunity to further grasp insight of self-awareness. Sometimes we experience a sense of emotional discomfort such as boredom, anxiety, fear, confusion or even social awkwardness. This can happen when we are in an environment that challenges our own comfort. Learning how to recognize these emotions can allow you to use them to be more productive. The goal is to recognize what your emotions are saying to you and transform them. Be careful to title it in your mind as healthy communication and not to label thoughts as "negative or positive" but instead "manage" translate them into positive tools for your benefit.

Key principles and points
> Emotional intelligence (EI) is the awareness of ones' own emotions as well as the emotional conditions of others around us.
> Fear is going to try to overturn your reasoning or any logical explanation. Keep pursuing something better.
> Beliefs control a majority of how we perceive everything.

> View emotions as advocates, and leverage emotions for your advantage

To leverage feelings for your benefit, you must become skilled in awareness. Awareness goes hand and hand with mindfulness. Our emotions do not occur without specific triggers. Each trigger induces a stage or shift in physiology followed by biochemical reactions in the brain. Each emotion has underlying beliefs that are associated with feelings we have.

Section Two: To Legacy - found by faithfulness: delivered by empowerment.

I want to provide a brief recap of everything up until this point.

Chapter One Identity: You have the authority to define who you are called to be. You don't have settle for life in the box. God created you to be authentic, empowered, courageous, and victorious. Use the tools necessary to develop the greatest sense of clarity in whom you are called to become.

Chapter Two Vision: Cultivate the greatest vision that aspires you to move forward. Don't settle in life. Use the power of visualization and imagination to break the barriers of scarcity and limited thinking. Take massive action of the things that fulfill who you are. Memories hold people in the past while vision propels others towards their defined state of fulfillment.

Chapter Three Mindset: Condition your mindset for progression. One of the world's leading photo corporations Kodak had digital technology before anyone else but they refused to innovate their business model. While everyone else moved forward they decided to stand firm to their modern beliefs. It cost the company everything. Everyone else moved to digital while Kodak went bankrupt. This is what happens when we fail to adopt a growth mindset. Challenge limited beliefs and anything that causes you to become stagnant.

Chapter Four Emotions: take inventory to understand your emotions. What environments bring you the most passion for life? Evaluate the triggers that cause stress, worry, anxiety, and fear. Carefully evaluate the beliefs associated with these current emotions. When you feel fearful reframe it and question whether the fear is a legitimate threat or an inaccurate perception based on a conditioned belief. Reshape how you view pain like the karate guru that chops bricks. Own your emotions through meditation.

Now it's time to journey to newness for God has called you to more than mediocrity. Let's go Chapter Five: Principles of intentionality.

To Legacy

We will now explore the power of being intentional. This involves accountability and stewardship of our identities, vision, mindsets, and emotions. Channel these four paradigms and explore the power of newness. Eliminate everything that is counterintuitive or not in alignment with your higher self. You will need to be focused, specific, and grounded on a foundation of excellence.

My life shifted the day I recognized I could become every hero I admired. When this occurred, I knew with time, I could shift my belief system to achieve even the most difficult task if I put in the effort, energy, and precision. I knew I could accomplish whatever I wanted with the favor of God, and with His love and grace. This is same for anyone who believes.

Remember, you have the authority to define who you are called to be. You don't have to settle for life in a box. God created you to be authentic, empowered, courageous, and victorious. Use the tools necessary to develop the greatest sense of clarity about who you are called to be.

Cultivate the greatest vision that aspires you to move forward. Don't settle in life. Use the power of visualization and imagination to break the barriers that point to scarcity and limited thinking. Take sacrificial action to fulfill your dreams and unleash your greatest self. Understand that memories hold people in the past, while vision propels others towards goal fulfillment.

Condition your mindset for progression. Challenge limited beliefs and anything that causes you to become stagnant. Take inventory to understand your emotions. What environments bring you the most passion in life? Evaluate the triggers that cause stress, worry, anxiety, and fear. Carefully evaluate the beliefs associated with these current emotions. When you feel fearful reframe it and question whether the fear is a legitimate threat or an inaccurate perception based on conditioned beliefs.

Wandering generality poem

Affirmations I have you not
For I'm on a quest as an astronaut
The destination that do I lack
For I took a trip without a map
My dreams excite, while goals despair
Procrastinate I know it well
They told me that I need a plan
Ideas they come but then they ran
I ventured far my eyes did see
A land with treasure lies beneath
I searched with passion in need of wealth
I had no plans so none would fail
Distracted much, appointments filled
This life of mine I'll never live
I took a chance it caused me stress
If I had my GPS

CHAPTER FIVE: PRINCIPLE OF INTENTIONALITY

*The greater versions of who we
are lies beyond the things we fail
to do.*

Found by faithfulness

A well-known parable in the bible tells of a shepherd who has a hundred sheep. As he is taking care of the sheep he notices one of them has gone missing. He counts the sheep again to make sure one isn't hiding. Ninety-six, ninety-seven, ninety-eight, ninety-nine, okay, "Where has the other sheep traveled off to?" he asks himself. He was worried about the sheep and began to search everywhere. He looked near and far until he found the sheep, because his sole purpose and duty was to fulfill his divine calling.

When you lose something important how long do you search for it? The shepherd knew what he was looking for, and nothing was going stop him from finding it. In fact, the sheep was only found due his faithfulness. As we carry on through the next few sections, I want you to question exactly where your intentions are concentrated on in this season of your life.

Get Off the Hamster Wheel

We live a cycle of conditioned reruns until we die, I call it the hamster wheel. My goal on this journey is to inspire you to go against the grain. Get out of the box. This will require you take everything out of the box, yourself, your vision, and your beliefs.

Are you living in a hamster wheel? I was, in fact--- if I were to evaluate everything about my life it would reflect a continuous cycle of futile repetitiveness in all areas of my life. Those cycles affected me financially, mentally, and spiritually. I was living paycheck to paycheck, cycling the same thought patterns of poverty, struggle, and strife. I was bankrupt because of hatred and bitterness. These feelings kept me from showing and receiving compassion. I was not in good health, because I was indulging in late night burrito sessions and playing Madden football and call of duty. I was eating fried chicken every day because that's how I was raised. I was literally repeating generational patterns that had been detrimental to those I knew and loved. My relationships were toxic, and I was surrounded by individuals who had no desire to advance in life. I'm not trying to depreciate the value of my upbringing, I am simply acknowledging that many of my decisions were a result of recycled conditioning.

In all honesty, even my beliefs were in a hamster wheel. How many of us can be honest with this form of self-discovery? In most cases, we either point fingers or blame something on others, the government, our jobs, or we resolve issues by avoiding them all together. At any rate, those who succeed beyond the barrier of mediocrity accept their fair share of accountability and live out the path God set forth for them. Meaning they seize the day and take dominion over it and their own future.

Even though I wasn't taught how to achieve success, there is a plethora of successful information available almost everywhere we turn. While some refuse to invest in new learnings, others take advantage of opportunities and build legacies. Even if your environment wasn't conducive to success, you can still build a firm foundation for yourself and your family. Speaking of building, everything has a starting point, everyone has been an amateur at something at one point or another.

From birth we are taught to evaluate our self-worth based on school grades and averages. Our parents pay us well when we get good grades, and punish us for failing. School grade averages aren't always indicative of future projections when it comes to success. In fact, you could be led to believe that those who are the most prosperous in life had become successful by reading a bunch of books and attaining knowledge. The only thing that guarantees advancement is the information applied in life. Your grade point average in public schools don't limit your achievement, you must be able to stay the course.

I have seen some of the most educated people working for individuals without an education or degrees, but were experts in goal setting, planning, strategy, and work ethic. Deciding your sense of self-worth based on grade point averages will always lead to an inadequacy or unrealistic expectations. Does that mean if you scored low on an aptitude test that you are stupid? Of course not, multiple tests prove there are many different ways to learn. Some ways just work better for others. However, one thing holds true, those who are most successful have a keen sense of direction, clarity, execution, and they apply what they have learned.

I taught my students to aim high and focus on what brings them joy and where they can make the most significant impact. Having clear direction creates an optimistic mindset and enables you to see what's possible for your life.

This section will help you to focus on direction rather than traditional methodologies of old-fashioned educational systems.

Don't Decorate your Cubicle

Emotional intelligence creates awareness necessary for combatting instant gratification. In addition, procrastination can also keep us from our greatness. On one side we have instant gratification and on the other side, procrastination. Being aware of what we are exercising empowers us and gives us direction on how to leverage these conditions.

Emotions can prevent us from growth when we aren't unaware of our behaviors. If you are tired of your job or feel as if you were created for more, I encourage you to pick up my other book titled. "Don't Decorate your Cubicle."

It was May of 2016, and I had spoken with my wife many times about quitting the corporate world to pursue entrepreneurship full time. I was working more than 15 hours per day between my job and my business. I worked my full-time job and then went home to work on my business. Each month my wife adjusted the budget to prepare for the changes that were to take place when I quit. I had been on the job for five years, and each day, I dreaded going. I performed well, but was so stressed that I became sick. I could be enjoying Sunday at church and the thought of me having to go back to work on Monday instantly made me nauseous. For some reason I wouldn't quit the job. Though I felt deeply in my heart that I was created to do something completely different, each time I attempted to take the leap, I'd come up with an excuse. Have you ever felt this way?

Each month I found myself coming up with excuses and delaying the date that I would take *the leap*! January came, and I told my wife, "Let me get one more commission check." February came and I said, "Hey we had a great last month, let's keep on saving." Then March came, and my wife said, "Are you going to quit your job?" I said yes, let me get just a few more checks." Then came April...and May. In May I went to work, and I noticed my friend Connie's' desk decorated, it was nice. She had gold and silver trimmings with positive quotes around her desk, and a nice little plant to match the ambiance of her work area. I commented, "I love your cubicle. It's positive and peaceful. It's a small refuge." She responded, "Thanks, D.J, if you get some stuff *I can decorate your cubicle as well.*"

In all of my enthusiasm, I ran home to tell my wife. For months she had been talking to me about quitting the job. "Babe I think I want to decorate my desk at work. A nice plant to improve the ambiance. Connie said she would help," My wife responded, "You aren't even going to be there long. Don't decorate your cubicle! You are creating the expectation that you plan on being there forever. Babe, what are you afraid of hasn't God always provided?"

What a moment of clarity, I had been afraid to assume the position God said was rightfully mine! Remember when facing new challenges, leap and...don't decorate the cubicle!

Evaluate trends to make an impact

Human behavior always presents an opportunity to make an impact. The CEO of Amazon, Jeff Bezos recognized a trend in online spending through e-commerce. Mark Zuckerberg recognized a trend in how people connect socially through Facebook. Tai Lopez recognized a trend in helping others become successful through online social media, investing, and podcast. How can you position yourself for growth while helping others achieve a positive outcome?

Some ways may include financial market and investing, selling products through e-commerce, recognizing the rising need for baby boomer support, or advertising through social media. Other ways may be through developing advertisement and marketing brands to build economic wealth or investing in healthcare. God gives us more than enough knowledge and instructions on how we can best serve others. We are often programmed to find success through traditional methodologies that produce little to no value at all.

I spent many years intensely focused on developing the highest grades rather than investing in understanding human behavior. Human behavior drives everything around us, the way we think, act, and what motivates us emotionally. If you recognize an unmet need you will always have direction on how to improve your life and others. If you have insight on creating value for others you will never go broke.

Following the traditional approach to success requires you attend school for twelve to sixteen years, work in a desired field for thirty years, and then retire in your golden years. Most people end up with a ton of debt, unfulfilled purpose or a desire to pursue their dreams. I found value in an approach by Author Emily Esfahani[18] in her book, *The Power of Meaning: Creating a life that Matters.*

Based on her book, the people that have the most fulfillment in their lives acquire the following keys:

- Belonging
- Purpose
- Storytelling
- Transcendence

---

[18] Emily Esfahani Smith is a writer in Washington DC. Her book *The Power of Meaning* was published in 2017 by Crown and has been translated into 16 different languages

These four pillars allow an individual to acquire a life of joy, meaning, fulfillment and purpose. This encompasses the embodiment of psychology from an internal and external perspective, and also creates a sense of direction. Our livelihood is based on a craving to belong. When we are first introduced to the world, even as infants we desire the attention of our parents, siblings, and family.

Implement the four keys Esfahani suggested by answering the questions below:
Belonging: Where can you find your niche to serve?
Purpose: What purpose, meaning, or cause can you devote your gifts, time, or talent to?
Storytelling: How can this contribution enhance your story and the story of others?
Transcendence: What areas can you invest in that will allow you to build an eternal impact?

Build your Passion with Purpose

My gifts haven't always been used in the most appropriate way. In my youth, I made music for fun and sometimes for my ego and popularity. As I matured, I recognized the value and impact of communication and words. They can tear down, or they can heal. The same mouth that built a legacy can ruin a lifetime of achievements, trust, value, and integrity. This is ever present in times where credible public figures lose all they have accumulated over something they said or did. It completely diminishes their character and brand. Even in my own life I have said and done things that I may never be forgiven for. We must guard our gifts, character and proceed through life with the utmost respect for the life we will have, even if we can't see it yet.

When God gave us gifts, his intentions weren't to see us stash them. He never intended for us to hide them. That's why they are called gifts. They are meant to be given to others. As a Master allowing someone else to watch his home while he was gone, he has entrusted us with his property to steward. What we do with it can bring hope and change the future of the world. I never thought I would be focused on music, speaking to youth, or hosting fundraising events. I have worked hard to build awareness about human trafficking and suicide. You must live this life to please God and help others. God created us to be the light in the world.

Build a Roadmap

A roadmap has great value and importance, because it allows us to shape the reality and to think more about what is possible for our lives. Sometimes we become bound to mediocrity because we don't have a roadmap that shows us what success looks like.

Each decision you make is a stroke of art on your canvas, why not make it look like the ideal portrait that will amaze you and others for generations to come. If God said, he came to earth so you could experience abundance--- **YOU** need to determine what that looks and feels like. In most cases, the time comes when we as adults get to decide what we want to experience. We get to choose whether that is abundance or hardship, peace or brokenness, lack or prosperity.

Create your own roadmap or bucket list, put your vision board on the wall, remind yourself that others have made it out. You already have great examples of those who have done what you are conspiring to do! Join their network, build a pipeline of resources, or a list of quality individuals you can add to your network. There are people out there who see you going places. Begin to use your G.P.S. *God Positioning System*. God knows best.

Proceed to appendix 5 for questions pertaining to chapter overview

CHAPTER SIX-THE POWER OF NEWNESS

Aspire to embrace a new mindset, and everything else will follow.

Nothing excites like the power of *new*. Getting a new car, new shoes, being in a new relationship, or even starting over to begin a new year is enough to make us exuberant. The truth is, it doesn't matter how new something is, nothing compares to a new mind, a new heart, a new beginning, or a new revelation. Exploring new heights and new limits within yourself creates greater possibilities, which means greater impact.

When God unfolds his vision for our lives, it is as if we are transitioning through a metamorphosis of evolutionary growth. To go from being an *average* person with no purpose, vision, identity, hope, mission--- to someone with a new mindset is amazing.

When these type of changes occur in our lives, people who knew us before notice the changes in us. This type of "looking different" is not like you got a haircut or your hair dyed, had plastic surgery or even lost a ton of weight. These kinds of changes are substantial. The type of change I'm speaking of is one that let's everyone know there has been a paradigm shift. And, in this shift all of your old beliefs are disposed of and the nature of God takes over your subconscious mind until you finally transition into the beauty you were created to become.

Sometimes individuals are okay with *nothing happening*. We should never want to settle for a "fixed" anything. Not a fixed mindset, fixed income or fixed relationship except in a marriage of course. That's probably why many of us have such a flawed perception of life. Prolonging the idea of your evolution will cause you to live in a state of dependency.

He wants our hearts and eyes constantly on him, so he can manifest what he desires for our lives.

My prayers for you is that your life will be so amazing that you astonish yourself. Working towards a higher version of yourself will require you to be uncomfortable at some point. Aspire to embrace a new mindset, and everything else will follow.

Say this out loud: I want to experience growth in every area of my life. I want to continuously astonish myself. I want to grow deeper in love with God, my spouse. I want to achieve goals. I want to evolve until God calls me home.

Now, don't be ashamed to be peculiar. You were created to complement the culture not to conform to its standards. I began to study new environments, to adopt new philosophies and empower myself by being around other like-minded individuals who inspired me to thrive in life. Before I knew it, I was going back to show some of my friends how to do the same.

Paradigms

If order for the results of compounding to take place, YOU **MUST** take ACTION. Even small snowballs over time create avalanches.

It is said that human beings are habitual, mainly because our mind seeks to familiarize our existence through a routine. It is as if our brains are computer programs. The system navigates through algorithms that only change if we intentionally shift. Isn't it interesting that we naturally sit in the same spot when we go to a place we are familiar with? We tend to park in the same parking spots at work. When we get dressed in the morning, we begin with the same regimen every day. Nothing really changes.

If we are indeed a result of the routines we adopt, why not select a model or method that strengthens our identity? Each person is a mere reflection of their habits. Like my fitness coach Cody Madison says, "The first meal of the day tells your body whether to store fat or burn calories." What system of operations are you setting your body up for? Is it mediocrity or building legacies?

Every successful person has a routine or a ritual for success and breakthrough. Our lives often play out like an algorithm; a set of patterns, habits, rituals, or behaviors that have the capability to produce results. The only difference between mediocre and achievement is the set of patterns that distinguish the two. Successful people intentionally choose patterns that are in their best interest and those that achieve optimal results. The problem is our brains are wired to select the path of least resistance, therefore we naturally select comfort. This becomes a state of confinement. **In other words, when we live in default mode we are not active advocates in the creation of our dreams**. This should be a non-negotiable. You can condition your mind to seek opportunities or you can condition your mind to embrace negativity or reject self-doubt. You can set your mind to recognize abundance or expect poverty. Before I knew God, I was stuck. I didn't realize there was no such thing as barriers when you serve a **breakthrough** God!

Create a daily ritual to recondition your heart, mind, and soul!

Picture your mind like a highway. On the highway there are many different pathways, avenues, lines of traffic, exits, barriers, and directions that lead to ongoing traffic. This reminds me of a time, my wife and I were conversing about people who impede traffic or drive slow in the passing lane preventing others from passing them. This delays traffic altogether. Isn't that annoying? Well, depending on how you start your day you could do be doing the same exact thing! You could be impeding your own progress by **not** conditioning your mindset correctly. Conditioning your mind to establish new, healthy habits will significantly advance your life.

In order to maximize prosperity, growth, and evolution you must have a *GAMEPLAN*.

Gratification: Gratitude is the highest state of consciousness, it opens our hearts to give and receive. In defensive mode, we automatically start the day focused on everything that could go wrong. It's time to counter that natural tendency to complain. When I wake up in the morning, I thank God. I find at least five things to be thankful for. I have a large eraser board in my house and on it is written "What you are grateful for?" I automatically want to focus on all of the things that I am proud of and grateful for. This brings me to a place of worship, and if you do this, it will place your mind in an elevated state of consciousness. When you wake up with your mind focused on your blessings, it starts and ends in a positive manner and open pathways for love and grace to flow freely.

Affirmation: It is time for a renewal. It is times to declare the beauty you were created for. You are a King or Queen. This should be in your affirmation. Declare your greatness and pray God opens avenues that allow you to witness how amazing you are to Him as His child. Your inner talk dictates your outer reality just like your mindset illustrates your perception of reality. The only words you should speak are those that edify and uplift yourself and others.

Meditation: I am pretty new to meditation, but I am a seasoned prayer warrior. Both operate within the same perimeter of the mind while inducing our thoughts and perceptions to a peaceful state. Meditation clears out the negativity and opens up your mind to receive positivity and clarity. Listen to music or something that inspiring to you to direct the traffic for the day. Pray, press play, praise God, and press through for your break through.

Exercise: I wish I could tell you with great confidence that if you have a sharp mind you will have a healthy body. This isn't always the case. We live in a society that recognizes all types of harmful things, but many of us haven't taken preventive measures to be healthy. Many people are still eating meats that are packed with hormones or overindulging in alcohol. Exercise is important for your mind, body, and heart and ensures it will be in the best condition. If you exercise you get better results, live longer, and feel better.

Plans or Goal: Think about how you have planned your life out so far, your week, and your day. Review your goals for this season. What is your vision? Are you doing what God has called for you? What is inspiring you to dominate your goals and your vision?

Lessons learned: Learning empowers you to grow and bring others along on your journey. As leaders, we should be learning every day. What was the outcome of the previous day, week, or month? What lesson did you learn?

Aim for progress: What is one thing you can focus on that would greatly improve your life? Maybe you could spend less time on emails and focus on relationship building. Or perhaps you can invest more time reading, or maybe you should focus more in your health or finances. Pick one and aim.

Newness: God desires that all things be made new in our lives. Pray that someone else hears the message of the gospel. Pray for your salvation and the salvation of others. Regardless of where you are in life, God has a plan and a purpose for you. Let us all walk in newness by becoming the best versions of ourselves. Let us commit to breaking down the barriers that have been holding us back. How can you focus on becoming all God intended?

How do you start your day? Do you start your day with affirmations? Do you read scriptures to get closer to God? Are you listening to gossip or filling your mind with literature that inspires you to expand to new heights? Studies show that the happiest people in the world are those who not only consistently explore new heights of success, but they challenge themselves to grow daily. What was your last great achievement? How can you improve your life and behaviors to uncover your true self and to become the person you were meant to be?

We tend to choose things that are destructive to our character and to our lives. My mother calls it "selling the car for gas money." Making short-term decisions without recognizing the long-term impacts is probably one of the most harmful decisions that hurt us, but it is deciding to be disciplined every day that lead to newness.

First, you need a system and order of operation. The Lord says in the bible that he orders our steps, which means God is very much systematic. He is very capable of bringing order to our chaos.

What you can accomplish by sacrificing an additional 30 minutes each morning:

- ➢ Take five minutes and write an affirmation that affirms who you are and why God created you).
- ➢ Meditate for 10 minutes, thank God the creator for his grace and mercy.
- ➢ Read the bible for 10 minutes.
- ➢ Listen to something motivational for 5 minutes.

If you create new habits, old habits will die. You have now committed to consuming new information. Becoming an expert reveals your constant effort to renew yourself. Following this pattern will restore your mind, body, and soul. Choose a paradigm that best suits you.

Commit to your expectations

People who actually reach their potential are far and in between. Success for most is rare. Think about it, how many people do you know who have actually reached their *full* potential? Potential requires self-esteem and confidence in order to evolve. Most people have either no confidence or their confidence is under developed. Confidence can be boosted over time by sharpening gifts and talents, with familiarity of a subject, and through prayer and meditation.

Confidence, courage, and execution confronts fear, but most often we are led to give up when we face any form of adversity. We are most astonished when we achieve things outside of what we believe we are capable of. While the average does the bare minimum, those who excel to greater heights recognize the importance of committing to standards that stretch them. You don't have to worry about expectations that others have of you, if you have high expectations for yourself. That's that *newness* talk.

Use the Power of Compounding

If you were to get hit with a snowball, it wouldn't cause much of an impact at all. In fact, more than likely you would brush it off as no big thing because the size of the small ball is insignificant and would result in minimal injury. Now, if you were to get hit with numerous amounts of snowballs all at once, there may be some trouble there, because this my friend is called an avalanche! This is the power of compounding.

Albert Einstein calls compounding the 8th wonder of the world. There is no power on earth like compounding. To provide an example, I will display a demonstration of compounding below. In the financial realm it's called compound interest which is a universal law.

If I were to offer you a million dollars today or the sum of a penny doubled every day for thirty-one days which one would you accept? Most likely you would be tempted to receive the million dollars, but anyone who knows the power of compounding interest is aware that after thirty days that a penny doubled over time becomes five million dollars. Or, if you wait in thirty-one days it becomes ten billion dollars! I was in just as much disbelief when I first heard of this concept, so I had to include it here for your reference.

Day	Value	Day	Value	Day	Value
1	$0.01	11	$10.24	21	$10,485.76
2	$0.02	12	$20.48	22	$20,971.52
3	$0.04	13	$40.96	23	$41,943.04
4	$0.08	14	$81.92	24	$83,886.08
5	$0.16	15	$163.84	25	$167,772.16
6	$0.32	16	$327.68	26	$335,544.32
7	$0.64	17	$655.36	27	$671,088.64
8	$1.28	18	$1,310.72	28	$1,342,177.28
9	$2.56	19	$2,621.44	29	$2,684,354.56
10	$5.12	20	$5,242.88	30	$5,368,709.12

What does this have to do with newness? Each decision we make compounds over time, so the smallest decisions over time compound to make the most significant impacts. This works in two directions, whether negative or positive.

You can buy one share of stock and it can compound into millions of dollars or you can buy liabilities and it can compound into debt. You can invent in one new skill and overtime be an expert or you can spend your time doing the same old routine and have nothing to show for your life. You can eat junk food and have near death experience or change one eating habit and be in the best shape of your life in as less as ninety days. No manner what decision you make it will compound.

Walking in newness takes discipline. Imagine each decision you make creating a snowball effect. This is what I do to stay disciplined. This along with tracking and accountability leads to transformations. As you can see, one small change can lead to big gains in the end.

Upgrade your belief system

If you study the minds of some of the greatest that ever lived you can understand how to triumph when most have failed; and you will be equipped to overcome when most have failed. If you model the behaviors of some of the greatest minds that have ever lived, people around you will clearly witness that you're thinking, acting, and living your best life--- out loud. And, you are doing it just as some of the greats did, with incredible fortitude.

By now we have talked a lot about mindset. Now, I want you to channel your energy towards learning and spending time to adopt philosophies of others who think on a higher level of consciousness than you. This requires emotional intelligence. You must be able to recognize when you are becoming uncomfortable, and have the mindset to successfully do this. This ultimately requires stepping out of your comfort zone. Courageous fortitude is your best advocate for taking on adventures that seems risky. If you feel afraid, just do it anyway. Hang around people that have accumulated so much that it makes you feel insecure. Invest in people that think on such a higher level that it causes you to break the bondages of your own thinking. **Osmosis is the only cure for brain power deficiency or being raised in a toxic environment that has poorly impacted our conscious minds**. Associations by great people challenge the frequency of your thought patterns. This may be the only thing that saves you from yourself.

I learned about identity from studying Steve Biko. I learned about wealth from reading books by Napoleon Hill, Brian Tracy, and Dennis Kimbro. I learned about mental toughness by attending seminars hosted by Steve Siebold. I learned the art of compassion by reading over Thich Nhat Hanh, Martin Luther King Jr., and many others. I learned much about leadership from John C Maxwell and T.D

Jakes. I learned goal setting and business from Grant Cardone. I learned self-development from one of my favorite speakers, Les Brown.

Nothing elevates our beliefs like challenging the patterns in which we think. One of the greatest blessings God gives us is the ability to enhance how we think about ourselves and others. How can you grow in value if you aren't investing in yourself?

Some say, we should only hang around individuals that think like us, act like us, or have the same visions and aspirations that we do. I challenge you to only hang around people who encourage you to level up. Go to a different country, explore different methods of living, study other religions and cultures to find the beauty in others and learn from people who think on higher frequencies than you. This should be a group that holds you accountable while inspiring your growth. If you love technology, seek out someone who is a subject matter expert. This is the difference between super achievers and those who are bound by mediocrity. Don't settle for being around people who think like you unless they are motivating you to try new and better things.

Do small things in a great way: you can't rush greatness!

When I hustled in the streets I hustled hard. I have an obsessive personality that enjoys doing everything over-the-top. Maybe it's the Leo or Alpha-male in me that desires to always go crazy! I go above and beyond in anything I do. If you are like me, then this section will be beneficial because I was a jack of all trades and master of none!

I'm a big fan of Grant Cardones' 10X philosophy, (aiming for 10 times more than your actual goal) the take massive action and achieve big goals, but God really challenged my heart regarding this approach to life. Most leaders will encourage you to run, run, run and race for your goal, but the individuals that are most influential take calculated and intentional steps. These small calculated steps have the biggest impacts on your *to-do-list*.

This section is simply meant to challenge you to create small wins throughout your day. Doing small things in a great way may require you to change the method in which you evaluate scheduling and life. If you are a high energy "get it done" type of person like me, small habits create massive behavior paradigms. Let your day be ruled with small wins and even schedule block each one. I'll give an example below. Let's talk pros and cons first.

- Mental aptitude
  - The mind is the most incredible tool you have, but it can also become over worked leading to mental fatigue.
  - Taking on more than one activity at once reduces attention span and allocates more awareness to certain engagements, increasing lost time and minimizing efficiency.
  - The brains' neuropathways become "strengthened" the more you focus on one area at a time.
  - Concentration improves as well as impression upon the subconscious mind to be fully functional, aware, engaged, and present in the area you are targeting as your legacy.
- Multitasking is a Myth
  - Research has shown that it takes an average of 45 minutes to regain concentration once it is broken.
  - While doing multiple projects at once distraction is more likely to occur through broken patterns of activity.

- Studies have shown trillions of dollars are being lost due to disengagement in the work place.
- Disengagement creates more stress on the body and mind.
- Balance
  - Doing small things provides greater sense of clarity on what's most important.
  - Doing small things allows you to operate in your lane.
  - Prioritization impacts efficiency.
  - Greater results are created.
  - Creates opportunities for everyone to win and improves your success rate.
  - Allows you to have more sustained energy throughout the day.
  - Builds more wins for you!

By setting small habits of focused and concentrated efforts each small decision creates long term big wins.

Stewardship

As long as the good Lord provides you oxygen, you will need to work toward building a legacy that astonishes the world. It is only through astonishment we can recognize the mark you were created to leave. Aspire towards extraordinary results! You are equipped to develop, called to steward, and expected to win, but will you answer the call of duty?

In the book we have spoken a lot about building legacy and even striving to get out of our comfort zone, but we haven't talked a lot about stewardship. If you have experienced some abuse then authority is probably not a word that you are fond of, because I despised authority growing up. I have been racially profiled, targeted, and even brutalized by corrupt police officers. I had been humiliated and beat by my father. I have even had money stolen by individuals I trusted. The rewards of guidance, accountability, and provision will always outweigh the losses you take in life. If you have the right support and guidance governing your actions you will have nothing to be concerned about.

Submission and direction

Accountability starts with submission and guidance. Submission starts with wise counsel or governing over ones' own aspirations with one goal in mind, success. Failure may occur, but with the right guidance you can become more efficient. Effective mentorship should be received from someone that has a track record of leading with high standards. As an example, for many years I struggled in many different areas, weight loss, pornography addiction, and alcohol abuse. I found a greater sense of relief allowing individuals into my life who were conscious of purity, righteousness, and self-discipline. Your desire to flourish must be greater than your desire for comfort. The greatest competition you'll face is overcoming the dysfunctions of self.

To some of my friends this is not an important task in their lives, so these are not the type of individuals I want providing counsel to me. Embrace people in your life who are strengthened in areas where you need improvement. Naturally, you will attract their characteristics and it will be evident in your own behaviors.

Submission

God recognized the value of order, structure, and authority, but growth can only happens in your life when you welcome it whole heartedly. As a parent and leader, I understand the value of submission. I have far more experience in my life than my children, but I also recognize my own short comings. I recognize that I am more prone to be comfortable than to challenge myself to higher standards. Submitting to someone wiser than us empowers us to grow stronger, wiser, and more effective. Wisdom comes from authority and is important for your development. Submitting under someone else's leadership allows your foundation to be strengthened. This is important in maintaining a sense of order to combat the chaos we manage daily. We all need someone we can be accountable to. Will you allow someone greater than you to lead you?

Stewardship

You may recall the parable in the bible about an owner who trusted his home to be watched over while he left on a trip. Anyone who would trust someone with their refuge must have high expectations and trust for that individual to leave his most esteemed possessions. You would only let certain type of people watch over your home, right?

Picture this scenario like the breath of oxygen God gives you. Each of us are living on *borrowed time* and soon the owner of the home will return--- waiting to see how we stewarded the gifts, talents, and time while He was away. The beauty of stewardship is you can "own" what is granted to you through accountability. God is asking you to be the gatekeeper and the governing body of stewardship. He isn't leaving without providing adequate and effective tools.

God is counting on you to build something monumental with great expectancy. He wants to see how you show up and show out in life. You are too important to be *good*, **you should be great.**

God wants you to experience abundance and live a full life of joy, passion, and hope. He has gone ahead of you and has already deemed you victorious. Will you walk forward to claim what he said was already yours? I don't care if you have to crawl, walk, roll, run, or tread I just want you to get there one step at a time.

We chose you poem

I sent you email after email, you never did respond though.
I figured you were busy giving lectures using wise quotes
Of all the times you failed, there was a story that you told
A group of talents looking for someone they could behold
The person they chose was charismatic and ambitious
Tall in stature, rich in beauty, but inside he lacked the vision
Still the talents were committed and they decided to stay
Hoping the time would come around that he'd be ready to create
Seldom chances came by, the talents began to talk
When the mentor saw the guy to tell him just what they thought
He asked what you want from life. He never pondered the question
The talents got excited, and the mentor made an impression
He said you were made for greatness, you have talents and you're gifted
Though you've had a rough past every challenge is a privilege
Deep inside you there's a passion... can you fathom what we're building
God has given you a purpose. Build a pathway to your vision
The talents were ignited as the man started to think...
Of all of his regrets over successes he had achieved
He started to lose focus of the things he believed
The talents tried to remind him to reinforce his self-belief
Soon enough the passion died along with promises he made
Cause he never took the time to chase the dreams he'd convey
But the talents didn't leave, and they decided to stay
As they talked among themselves from deep inside the grave,
Saying, "We chose you."

CHAPTER SEVEN: LIVING THE LEGACY

You have no idea who your evolution is called to reach. Commit to growing. Leave something bigger than yourself.

Signed, Legacy.

T he people with the biggest regrets in life are the ones with the best ideas they never acted on. Execution is key. Today is the first day of forever… I want to impress upon you to own it. Don't accept any identity but the one you feel worthy of accepting, that is the version of yourself you can be most proud of.

Take ownership of your destiny. You get one life, live your dreams. Take ownership of your mindset. Don't settle for thoughts that do not represent the excellence you seek and are called for. Take ownership of your emotions. Don't let your emotions drive you, leverage them to make the best impact you can. Build your legacy now. There is no opportunity like the present. Build equity and ensure you go for the gold.

The power of now carries a lot of weight. The hardest reality I've seen people face is regret. To know they could have had a better life, but wasn't all in, is a hard pill to swallow. To know they didn't give everything they were capable of giving for the sake of achieving their dreams isn't easy to live with. To know that God invested talent, time, energy, and potential into you, and yet you didn't aspire to reach your greatest potential, would be tough for anyone.

My prayers are that you never know the feeling of regret. So, in the final chapter, we will discuss your expectations, how you can accomplish the desired result, and manifest necessary pathways to your dreams. Think about this for a moment:

You're sitting in a dark room unable to see, rendering your sense of sight ineffectual. You are incapable of making out any objects in front of your face, because you are blind. Cognitive behaviors lead you into seeking a source of light. You are aware that light is the source that allows you to see in the presence of darkness. Why do you believe that just because you flip a light switch, the light will come on? It is because of the trust factor *and your faith* that the light has always come on when you flipped a switch.

Think about this, its leg day, and your body is fatigued, your legs are sore, and you just so happen to you see a place to sit. Sitting would relieve some pressure. What is your next move? You're going to take a seat in that chair, right? But why do you believe this chair is going to support your weight? Just like the light bulb the chair has a sense of familiarity as well. There is a rational expectation that tells you this has always worked and it will work this time as well. It takes faith to have these expectations.

The thing that separate individuals who operate with a mediocre mindset from super-achievers is expectancy. Certain individuals pursue goals with expectations of winning, and they are driven to do so, because of familiarity. When you pursue something with expectations and faith, your emotions radiate that. There is a frequency that moves through your heart, mind, body, and soul. All of your concentrated efforts will persist in a focused manner maximizing your chances to achieve the desired outcome.

This manifestation principle was given to me when I won a contest a few years ago. It has been a daily ritual of mine ever since I first heard it. When I plan my day, I speak my truth into existence, because I believe I was created to conquer. So, the expectations must be aligned with the desired perception if it is to be manifested.

This may sound cocky, arrogant, or unrealistic, but if we were to observe the standard expectations many of us have, we could automatically tell our dreams are much greater than our expectations. Our expectations tend to be much lower than our potential. You should always expect much more, and execute higher. Confidence in yourself and your ability to drive beyond the norm can make a difference in your survival. Your mindset is the only thing standing between you and your dreams. And while you may have experienced a past of misfortune, this doesn't have to be your future. You could very well be the one God is calling to break generational curses in your family.

There's a difference between playing a game like you have won before and playing like you are *called* to win. Wh*en you are called to win* you modeled behaviors that are *congruent* with your expectations.

Buster Douglas knew when he stepped in the ring with Mike Tyson he had won already. He drew passion from his mother's death to acquire a win, but it was his expectancy that fulfilled the manifestation. He visualized it, spoke it, meditated on it, and delivered what he had seen in his mind. The fight was won before he even stepped into the ring. Muhammed Ali was known for preparing for his battles in the same exact manner.

Some people play like there's potential to win and there's the other kind of people. The "Burn the boat," "No plan B," "All or nothing" breed of human beings that put everything up, and would lose it all --- including their existence to achieve their desired outcome. This is how Jesus delivered salvation to mankind, he was willing to lose it all. There is nothing mediocre about a God that sacrificed His life to save humanity. We, as his children should aspire to emulate that.

Be the Minority, Expect to Win

If you have listened to Jim Rohm or Earl Nightingale, you're familiar with this statement. "If you were to ask a group of ambitious twenty-five-year-olds how many will be achieving their dreams before they die, most likely there would be a room full of hands in the air, however, studies show that out of one hundred people only 5% actually achieve their dreams.

This can be viewed in multiple ways. You can say that 95% of the people decided to conform to behavioral patterns that weren't conducive to success, or only 5% had what it took to achieve what they found worthwhile. You and I may have different definitions of success, so what you find worthwhile may be different than what I perceive as fulfillment. Earl Nightingale describes success as a progressive realization of a worthy idea.

Many of us show up with no expectations, no focused concentration, and no specific aim, therefore we are still bound to mediocrity. Each of us are accountable for the results we reap in life. Although each day presents new challenges we are equipped to live out a purpose driven life.

Create expectations based on your desire to win

Most people won't test drive a car without expecting to purchase it. So, why do people live life without expecting to win? When you have a car in mind, you visualize it, and then you do your research. Most people go online to search for deals and look at the blue book for the car's value. Then think hard and long about what they are willing to pay. If you are in the market for a car, you go to the dealership in search of what you want.

Once you see the car, you get in it, your hands touch the steering wheel, you get a feel for the seating to see how well the quality and comfort is. You then picture yourself driving in the car with family and friends. You adjust the seating and make sure the air conditioning and other features work. You make sure this is what you want to invest in. This is how we should test drive life!

God told Abram to leave his place of birth to venture into unknown territory (Genesis 12 NIV). When Abram left Harran, the place of his birth, he was seventy-five years of age. God asked Abram to come to this foreign location with desired expectations of making him great. It was a location he had never in his life been exposed to. Yet, God had called Abram out of his comfort zone.

God will call you out of your comfort zone

When Abram reached this destination, God began to speak life over him saying, "I will make you a great nation, and I will bless you; I will make your name great, and you will be a blessing. I will bless those who bless you, and whoever curses you I will curse, and all of the peoples on earth will be blessed through you." (Genesis 12:4 NIV).

When Abram went to the foreign land, God advised him to scope it out. Before Abram had children, he told Abram this is where your offspring will live. God was showing Abram the projections for his life. (Genesis 12:6). Just like test driving a car, God was showing Abram how to manifest the calling on his life. He asked him to go throughout the land, and look at it inch by inch, "Tell me what you see. What type of future do you see for yourself?" He associated greatness with Abram's name. God was preparing Abram's mindset and expectations for what was ahead.

You may recall, Abram jumped the gun and went ahead of God. He didn't see how God would make him a father of many nations. He was a hundred years old, and his wife Sarai was barren and couldn't have children. After

God reminded him of the promise, Sarah had a child, and God changed both his and Sarai's names to signify the calling he had on their lives. Abram was changed to Abraham and Sarai was changed to Sarah meaning "father and mother of many nations." From them, kings and queens were born.

Abraham and Sarah didn't conform like the majority of individuals, they stood firm. This is what separated the 5% from the 95% that Earl Nightingale spoke of. You are called to make a huge impact. Today you are putting penmanship to the subconscious mind to communicate a desired state of consciousness.

What will people say about you after you are gone? What achievements do you want to be known for in the next five, ten, twenty years? What experiences do you plan to have under your belt? What are your aspirations? (Examples could include real estate mogul, self-published bestselling author, national television syndicate, doctor or CEO of a nonprofit, or school teacher).

Write a testimonial letter from someone who greatly benefitted from you pursuing your dreams. This should be something that will lead to a sense of urgency for fulfilling your dreams and goals. If you are a future author write a third person testimonial about how *your book* inspired others. If you plan to be a doctor write a letter from a patient who you helped in the *future*.

Individuals who don't get outside the scope of their comfort zones or take risks in life are more likely to live with the biggest regrets. The person who never started the business they dreamed of, the student that never completed the education they once attempted, the author that never finished the book they wanted to write, or the artist who never recorded the song, missed a critical contribution that could have had the capacity to completely alter the future of generations.

What if Martin Luther King Jr. never delivered a speech, or if Steve Biko never revolted or if Nelson Mandela decided to continue being a lawyer instead of standing up for racial injustice? Those individuals are all well known for their resilience and the impact made. They are icons because they completed their life's mission even when faced with adversity.

Write the testimonials as if they are already complete. Write your goals as if they are already complete. Create expectations as if they are already fulfilled. Don't leave room for doubt and discouragement. You are here to leave a mark on earth. What will people say about you? What do you want to be known for?

I remember having to write a report about my great-grandfather. There was a problem though, I didn't know my great-grandfather. The vision my great-grandfather had for his life wasn't strong enough to build a lasting legacy. What will your great grandchildren say about you?

Imagine it's ten, twenty, thirty, or even forty years later in the future. Your great grandchildren are responsible for writing a paper about the impact you made. What will they say about you and your legacy? What will they be most proud of? What challenges will they say you overcame? What impact will you have made in the family? How will they celebrate you?

Live life with no regrets

If you died today what would be your biggest regret?
-Cody Bobay

Do you have any regrets at all? I know I have plenty of them. If you have none, perfect! If you have one or a few write it down on paper and let's deal with it. Having faced sad situations such as infidelity, child custody cases, and trouble with law enforcement, I'm grateful to have experienced the work of building my character. I wish I had received God sooner. I had two children out of wedlock that I love dearly, but it wasn't until I learned that God had a plan for my life that I began to really love and value the man I am today.

Time is but a vapor and knowing that alone should inspire us to value people and eliminate regrets. It should also inspire us to make the most of the time we have. Those who are most influential, discipline themselves well with the very thought of time. They maximize their effort during each moment they are gifted with. Once you remove guilt and regret you can start to put all your energy towards the things that matter most.

A guy I am mentoring spent close to twenty years in prison. Though he served his time and was able to start over he still had regrets of time missed with his children. After listening to his story, I reminded him of all the success he is now experiencing. He has an excellent paying job, is newly engaged with a great support system, and has been attending and now ministering to others about overcoming barriers. His spirit was still broken over the resentment felt by his children. Some things we can't repair no matter what we do, the past will come and go, but we can work to make a difference.

No one is known for the things or words they utter, but for the actions they execute. Don't be bound by the past when the future has plans for you. If your life is full of regret it is time to rewrite the script. We all face challenges in life. Some result in victory, while others result in misfortune, either way--- as long as we have breath in our bodies we are all given the opportunity to rewrite the script.

What changes do you want to live out from this day forth? Think about what you would say in a letter to your *future* self. What are some of the points you would make? Last and final, what narrative do you want remembered on your dash?

The Dash

One thing we all have in common is birth and death. It's something we can't escape. No matter where you run, you are bound to run into it. The beauty of the events that take place between birth and death is called the dash, it is that little symbol that indicates what took place while we were here on earth.

The dash is the life I remembered my mother for. The unlimited contributions she gave through the lasting talks and discussions we held. The talk we had when we experienced trauma and how we couldn't allow setbacks to be the final position of our lives. The dash represented the many times my sisters and I went out with her to spend time together as a family. We laughed at old memories, and these joyful moments have surpassed any moment or situation. Holding on to what matters most and using that to fuel your passion is vital. My mother always had scriptures that she held on to even before she died.

I encourage you to write a mantra, one that will highlight the impact you want to make in your dash. Let your mantra be a reminder that all things including *you* can be made new:

Remember there are people who merely exist, but not everyone lives. What is life if you haven't achieved the mission set forth for your destiny? Let that be a question that guides you on this journey called life. Go and build your own legacy. Being a creator is your divine duty of excellence. Peace.

Notes and appendix

Appendix section 1

Here are some personality assessments to take. One of the greatest forms of self-awareness takes place during discovery. What are some of your strengths, weaknesses, and opportunity for growth? How can you use this information to build your own uniqueness?

<u>Free personality assessment</u>

1. https://www.truity.com/test/holland-code-career-test
2. https://www.16personalities.com/free-personality-test
3. http://you.visualdna.com/quiz/whoami#/quiz
4. http://www.testcolor.com/personalitytest/personalitytest.php
5. http://www.seemypersonality.com/IQ-Test
6. https://www.funeducation.com/Tests/IQTest/TakeTest.aspx
7. https://www.skillsyouneed.com/ls/index.php/343479/lang/en/newtest/Y

What are some things that shape your values? What are your aspirations? What are some of your passions and obsessions? Did the results align with the pathway that you are currently pursuing? Why or why not?

Appendix section 2

Fill in the blank.
1. The ideal life I want for myself looks like _____.
2. Events, hobbies, or activities that fuel my enthusiasm include_____.
3. When people think me, I want to be known for____.
4. The vision I want for my life includes _____.
5. The vision for my life shows that I value _____.
6. What areas or field of expertise brings you the most fulfillment?

7. If you were given $30,000 to quit your job for 3 months, what would you do?

Appendix section 3

1. What kind of ideal mindset do you want for your life?
2. What are some limited beliefs you have about yourself?
3. What are some experiences that trigger negative thoughts about yourself or others?
4. Do you have a fixed or growth mindset?
5. What impact does limiting beliefs have on your life?

Appendix section 4

Answer the following

- Times when I am at peace the most are:
- Environment that cause me the most stress involve:
- The moments I experience the most joy includes:
- I am most fulfilled when I am doing:
- I feel good about myself when:
- The periods when I am in complete bliss looks like:

Appendix section 5

Belonging: Where can you find your niche to serve?
Purpose: What purpose, meaning, or cause can you devote your gifts, time, or talent to?
Storytelling: How can this contribution enhance your story and the story of others?
Transcendence: What areas can you invest in that will allow you to build an eternal impact?

1. Are there any mindsets you are recycling that has you stuck on the hamster wheel?
2. In what areas are you bound financially, spiritually, mentally, or physically that you need to break through?
3. How often do you serve others?
4. What are your beliefs about helping others?
5. What techniques do you use to create a sense of direction in your life?
6. What are some of the goals you are currently focused on?
7. Are you currently on the right path and moving towards a passion that motivates you?
8. If not, what exactly do you need to do to get on track?
9. Have you developed a roadmap that will direct and help to manifest your dreams and calling?

Appendix section 6

1. Is there any area of your life that needs to be made new?
2. What areas of your life need to be revitalized?
3. What type of accountability do you have in your life?
4. How can other individuals upgrade your belief system?
5. How are you managing your time?
6. Will you schedule time to honor God and the call He has on your life?

Appendix section 7
1. What will people say about you after you are gone? What achievements do you want to be known for in the next five, ten, twenty years? What experiences do you plan to have under your belt? What are your aspirations? (Examples could

include real estate mogul, self-published bestselling author, national television syndicate, doctor or CEO of a nonprofit, or school teacher).

2. What will they say about you and your legacy? What will they be most proud of? What challenges will they say you overcame? What impact will you have made in the family? How will they celebrate you?

3. Write a testimonial letter from someone who greatly benefitted from you pursuing your dreams. This should be something that will lead to a sense of urgency for fulfilling your dreams and goals. If you are a future author write a third person testimonial about how your book inspired others. If you plan to be a doctor write a letter from a patient who you helped in the future.

4. Imagine it's ten, twenty, thirty, or even forty years later in the future. Your great grandchildren are responsible for writing a paper about the impact you made. What will they say about you and your legacy? What will they be most proud of? What challenges will they say you overcame? What impact will you have made in the family? How will they celebrate you?

Foot notes

Page 13 Steve Biko https://www.biography.com/people/steve-biko-38884

Page 15-Cultural Anthropology Tracy Evans- Santa Ana College -
https://courses.lumenlearning.com/culturalanthropology/chapter/rite-of-passage/

Page 20-Gillian Lynne - Born To Dance Magically and Help Others Do the Same!
     Maggie Hofstaedter -
http://www.inspiremykids.com/2012/gillian-lynne-born-to-dance-magically-   and-help-others-do-the-same/

Page 38-Cognitive Dissonance
     https://www.psychologytoday.com/us/basics/cognitive-dissonance

Page 53- Abouthttps://drjoedispenza.com/pages/about

Page 69- George Washington Carver
https://www.biography.com/people/george-washington-carver-9240299

Page 75 -Aron Ralston - Epiphany Between a Rock and a Hard Place
     https://vimeo.com/3416326
Page 91- An Unhappy 'kodak Moment'
     Baltimore Sun -
https://www.baltimoresun.com/news/opinion/editorial/bs-ed-kodak-20120120-story.html

Page 100- Boundless Psychology
     Boundless -
https://courses.lumenlearning.com/boundless-psychology/chapter/introduction-to-consciousness/

Page 101-Sigmund Freud
https://www.biography.com/people/sigmund-freud-9302400

Page 108 Quantum Theory Demonstrated: Observation Affects Reality
https://www.sciencedaily.com/releases/1998/02/980227055013.htm

Page 110 -Growing Evidence of Brain Plasticity Michael Merzenich -
https://www.ted.com/talks/michael_merzenich_on_the_elastic_brain

Page 117- The Power of Emotional Intelligence | Travis Bradberry | Tedxucirvine TEDx Talks -
https://www.youtube.com/watch?v=auXNnTmhHsk

Page -118 The Reality of Imposter Syndrome
https://www.psychologytoday.com/us/blog/real-women/201809/the-reality-imposter-syndrome

Page- 123
https://www.psychologytoday.com/us/blog/contemporary-psychoanalysis-in-action/201609/what-is-healthy-narcissism

Page 133 Clinical Psychology
https://www.pearsonclinical.com/psychology/authors/rotter-julian.html Julian Rotter (born 22 October 1916) is an American psychologist who is known for developing influential theories, including social learning theory and locus of control.

Page 139 The Biology of Our Best and Worst Selves Robert-Sapolsky-
https://www.ted.com/talks/robert_sapolsky_the_biology_of_our_best_and_worst_selves?langu   age=en

Page 152 Emily Esfahani Smith http://emilyesfahanismith

About the Author

Donelle Cole is an effective communicator, mentor, financial coach and also an author. As an inspirer he lives to empower, equip, and uplift. He has a graduate degree in public administration and a bachelors in business. He served in the United States Navy, and is truly passionate about empowering others to live out their purpose to make an impact. As an entrepreneur he teaches others how to improve the quality of their life through seeking their God given potential. For more information please visit, Fromlivingtolegacy.com

CPSIA information can be obtained
at www.ICGtesting.com
Printed in the USA
BVHW061335270120
570620BV00016B/1447

9 781734 107708